Stop managing
time and start managing
your Energy!
all the Best

THE PRODUCTIVITY ZONE

Stop the Tug of War with Time

Penny Zenker

THE PRODUCTIVITY ZONE
Stop the Tug of War with Time
by Penny Zenker
with contributions from Megan Myers, PBC, MS

ISBN-13: 978-0986307508
ISBN-10: 0986307505
LCCN: 2014922291

Interior layout and design by Ellie Searl, Publishista®
Consulting editor -Alan Sharavsky
Final edits by Sarah Coolidge

SmartMoves Coaching, LLC
Devon, PA

Get your FREE
Productivity Accelerator Assessment

www.p10app.com

DEDICATION

I DEDICATE THIS BOOK IN memory of the two great men who strongly influenced both my outlook and my business results. First my father Carl Zenker, who passed away more than twenty-five years ago. When I was a child, my dad often had me help out in and around his office by adding up the ledgers, filing papers, and cutting the lawn. He taught me that earning money is easy when you fulfill a need and add value. I know he would be proud of me. I miss him. Second, Peter Hofer, the CEO of GFK Switzerland, who was my boss and mentor for seven years. Peter taught me that a great leader isn't there to motivate me, but to remove the obstacles that stand between me and my motivation.

Ultimately, I pursue this work for my children—for them to live life to the fullest and to achieve their hearts' desires. I want them to have their cake and eat it too! I want this for all children. When we live our lives in the Productivity Zone, we reduce stress, which has become one of the biggest obstacles to success and fulfillment.

CONTENTS

FORWARD

I FIRST MET PENNY AT CEO conference in Las Vegas in December 2014. I was one of the presenters and bumped into Penny by seeming chance. Of course, there really are no coincidences. There is a reason for everything. We spent some time chatting in a lounge area in the conference center. I was impressed by her intelligence, genuineness, and her sincere desire to make a difference in the world. She told me of her book and gave me a copy. Now I am privileged to write the forward for it.

I was intrigued right away by the title, *THE PRODUCTIVITY ZONE*, because I have been obsessed with productivity for decades. I have taught many seminars and have given many speeches on how to be more productive. The Productivity Zone and Penny's 10 Core Drivers of productivity are a fresh take on the productivity concept. It addition to what we normally think of as principles of productivity, like planning and prioritizing, she addresses the whole self, including the role of self-talk, state of your health, and language drivers.

I underlined the following from Chapter 4, *". . . your language defines, reveals and perpetuates who you are, not only to the rest of the world, but also to yourself."* There is so much power in that concept. I could go on because there are so many powerful principles covered in this book, but that would spoil the discovery process for you as you read the book.

Penny makes a bold promise that if you put into practice the 10 Core Drivers and stay in the Productivity Zone, your life will change for the better. You will think differently—you will become more productive, more successful, more balanced, and more in control. I can back up that claim. The concepts and principles shared in this book are tried-and-true, and if mastered, will do all that Penny says it will do.

Hyrum W Smith
Founder and Chairman of 3 Gaps
Founder, former Chairman and CEO of FranklinCovey

INTRODUCTION

M ANY OF THE EXECUTIVES WITH whom I work rate themselves as "very proficient" or at least an 8 out of 10 on their ability to manage their time. They are often surprised when they learn about the 10 Core Drivers and discover that they aren't scoring as high as they thought they would in at least a few of the elements. If I had a dollar for every time I've heard one of the executives say that they never realized all of the drivers contribute to productivity, I could retire on my own private island. The real excitement for me is seeing how much of a difference it makes in their lives and businesses when they start managing all the drivers that contribute to their productivity, rather than just the few they had previously been aware of. These executives have reported amazing shifts in their business and lifestyle as a result.

Your life will also be different in so many ways from this point forward. You will start to think of things from a new perspective when you evaluate the importance of tasks, goals, and strategies. You will ask new questions and be aware and more in control of your self-talk. You will achieve clarity quicker and be open to see more opportunities.

You will find that as you share these principles with others, and you will see the changes as they ripple through your home, your workplace, and your community. After implementing the 10 Core Drivers of productivity, my clients not only feel twice as productive, but also success comes easier and faster. They feel more balanced and in control.

One client, Dr. Isaac Jones, said after a session, "I will stand on my head if you tell me to because everything you coached me about was spot on." His business doubled in one year, and he had the systems in place to double it again year after year.

Don't worry, I won't have you stand on your head. The point is, these principles work. No matter the context, they WORK. When consistently applied they will work for you, too.

CHAPTER 1: WHERE WILL MY ARROW FALL?

S OMETHING HAD TO GIVE.

My heart was pounding, and I was sweating as if I had just run a marathon. For the third night that week, I was trading sleep for worry over paying my bills—which included the salaries of my two key employees, John and Sue. I mean, John had two kids who depended on him, and Sue was taking care of her elderly mom. I couldn't let them down.

From the moment I opened the doors of my company, cash flow had been a problem. Sure, I had recently closed some new projects. But one of my biggest clients hadn't paid his bills, and I was frantic. All my liquid assets were tied up in an ongoing project that I knew would have a big payout eventually. But "eventually" wasn't going to pay the bills NOW. Time was a luxury I didn't have. I was working seven days a week, and more often than not, sixteen hours a day. Every single pay period I went through the same panic: "Can I really ask my employees to be paid late? How long will they stay with me if I do? What will they think of me as a leader if I have to ask them to wait just one more week for their checks?" I was ashamed, frustrated, and stressed out. I hadn't paid myself in months. I was burning out fast, and deeply unhappy. The stress was affecting every aspect of my life.

What happened to the dream of flexible working hours and more freedom? Why did I feel more tied down than ever? I wished someone had told me this was the cost of owning your own business.

Something had to give.

———◆———

Entrepreneur Mindset

The truth is, I never intended to start my own business. I admit that I always valued money, probably more than my peers. Even as a child I was always involved in one "business venture" or another—lemonade stands, paper routes, mowing lawns—how ever I could serve a need and earn a dollar or two. But the difference between my friends and me was that I was usually doing all of those things every day, day after day—which meant I always had my own money to buy treats and toys or the spare cash to save for a rainy day. I didn't realize it back then, but I was enjoying creating my own opportunities and being my own boss.

As a young adult, I was open to any and all jobs. I worked the standard run-of-the-mill gigs: fast food counter girl ("fries with that?"), waitress, and six-foot sub builder. But I quickly learned that the more unusual options often proved to be the most lucrative—for example, delivering phone books for Donnelly directory. This was a workout and driving lesson all in one! I had to unload the truck, pack the car, and learn how to throw the directories while driving. I figured out a system to maximize the loading and delivery process to make more money in less time. Not only was I making more money being my own boss than I could working for someone else, I was having a blast doing it. During our senior year of college my best friend and I went into business selling welcome baskets to the parents of incoming freshman. After two semesters, we had raised enough money for an awesome trip to Europe!

It wasn't that I woke up one day and said to myself, "Today's the day I become an entrepreneur." Rather, it was a way of thinking. For me it was about finding places that I could add value. Even when I worked for other people, I approached my assignments as if it was my business on the line. I saw a lot of success that way and was quickly promoted through every company I worked for. By the time I was twenty-five, I owned my own IT company. Before I turned thirty-five, I had sold that business to a public company and was offered an executive leadership position at one of the top market research companies in the world. Of course, it wasn't all sunshine, rainbows, and smooth sailing. Anyone who has ever owned a business knows that there are good times and bad times.

➢ *It's what you do during the bad/hard times that defines and refines who you are.*

So Much to Do

Owning a business showed me that there was always more to do than could be done. On any given day, there were so many things to manage to keep clients happy and all the while deliver the value and standards that I prided myself on. Between supervising my growing staff, moving research and development further, and acquiring new customers to feed the pipeline, I felt that I could work 24 hours a day and still not gain traction. I always felt that if I could do one more thing, work one more hour, answer one more email, or call one more prospect, that's when I would finally get on top of things.

One night, after being awake for about thirty-six hours, having worked the last twenty or so days straight, I hit my breaking point. I was tired and couldn't do this any longer in this way. I mean, WHAT was I doing? I needed to take a step back, stop being busy, and stop working like a horse! I needed to start being productive and find more leverage. I needed to evaluate how I was working and redirect my focus on only those factors and activities that would magnify my results.

The signs were everywhere. My life was a mess. I wasn't eating right, I wasn't exercising enough, and my husband was getting sucked into the madness with me. The obvious question finally dawned on me: How effective could I possibly be if I was always running on empty? Was this what success was supposed to look like? I decided that I needed to stop blaming and start solving. Einstein said, "We can not solve our problems with the same level of thinking that created them."

It was time to change the way I was thinking and approaching the situation.

Take a Step Back and Look for Leverage

It took a few days for me to honestly assess how to get my company and my life in order. Staying away from the office those days was hard! In the back of my mind, I still heard the one-more-thing-gremlin whispering, "Get back to work." I was committed, however, to finding new ways of approaching my business and creating a new plan, so I changed my environment entirely and went away on a retreat. Three days later I was inspired, rejuvenated, and finally ready to pursue the success I knew the business was capable of. I completely overhauled what we focused on and how we operated.

Though I didn't realize it at the time, I was implementing my 10 Core Drivers of productivity. Long before I gave them a name, they were bringing me success. This was what helped me create the leverage to accelerate my company's growth. Two years later, I sold what had become a multi-million dollar company.

In Howard Pyle's famous adaptation of the Robin Hood folktale, "Robin Hood and His Merry Men," the hero shoots an arrow into the horizon, and with his dying breath declares, "Where the arrow falls, there bury me." Robin shot that arrow, but where it landed depended more on the wind than on him. Don't let yourself get caught in the trap of "letting the arrow fall where it may."

➢ *You can dictate your results, but only if you fully manage the factors that affect them.*

The Productivity Curve

Perhaps you're familiar with the Probability or Bell Curve. This describes the normal/average distribution of a large population of scores. Let's look at this famous curve in a new way.

This Productivity Curve is a visual depiction of the results you get based on what you do and how you approach what you do. This curve determines your level of personal productivity and satisfaction. The ends of the curve are outliers, or extremes. These are areas you want to avoid because the closer you get to them, the more your life is out of balance. It's at those corners where you'll allow yourself to make excuses. The goal is to reach the Productivity Zone where effective and efficient meet.

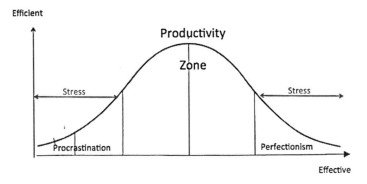

Procrastination

Look at the far left side of the curve. What you see are the people who aren't getting things done; they aren't accomplishing what they want. They're neither efficient nor effective. Maybe they're lacking clarity, or maybe they're stuck in complacency. Maybe they're unconsciously terrified of the very success they say they want. This is the environment that breeds procrastination.

There is a fine line between prioritization and avoidance. Priorities are usually the most important items, not the most urgent ones. A procrastinator's list is upside down, and they focus only on the urgent tasks, leaving the important ones to collect dust. However, it is these important tasks that really need doing, and by ignoring them, procrastinators remain stuck in place.

Procrastinators, being notorious excuse makers, keep important items on the bottom of the list and hone that craft over a lifetime. As a child, the budding procrastinator used the age-old, "The dog ate my homework" and from there the excuses got more sophisticated.

In an interview I conducted with John Perry, author of THE ART OF PROCRASTINATION, he spoke of the high levels of productivity that procrastinators think they have because of their urgency system. They get a lot done because the avoidance of high-risk important tasks frees them up to focus exclusively on the smaller low-risk tasks. Over time, those important tasks may become urgent and get done, but tasks typically don't get done until something else becomes more important. As Dr. Perry put it, "I can do anything, as long as there is something else more important that I ought to be doing."

Procrastinators are usually very busy, but no matter how much they actually accomplish, their stress levels are high, and their moods swing from apathy, to overwhelmed, to relief—while others sit in frustration. As a leader, this creates stress and later apathy at a lack of ownership in your organization.

Perfectionism

Now, consider the far right side of the curve. Those are the people who can't stop doing and doing and doing. They're the perfectionists, or what politically correct people would call "overachievers." Give them some credit: they are effective, they may even make a lot of money, but they are rarely efficient. Many entrepreneurs fall in this category; chances are YOU do too. Full disclosure: That's my Achilles heel. I still struggle with perfectionism from time to time. People on the overachieving side often fall into the trap of needing to do "just one more thing."

There is a fine line, however, between dedication and fixation. When you push and push, there's a breaking point where the price of "one more thing" becomes too great to ignore. Overachievers can get a huge number of things done. They may even make a lot of money. But typically, they aren't happy or fulfilled. And if you're not happy, are you really successful? Overachievers rarely give themselves the time to step back and enjoy what they've achieved. Sometimes, people become so addicted to the adrenaline rush and excitement of doing, and get so caught in the overdrive, they forget how to stop. They often forget or ignore their own needs. For these overachievers, the sense of purpose can be extremely strong. That purpose is the driving force behind their need to keep going. But this almost always ends in burnout, or missing out on the value and lessons along the way. Perfectionism is often a mask worn to hide the fear of not being good enough. Just like with procrastination, when you are caught up in perfectionism there will likely be collateral damage to those around you along the way. After all, if you live in a mental space of feeling like you are never good enough, how likely is it that someone else will measure up to your standards?

No matter where you typically fall on the curve, you're likely to slip into one of the other zones at one time or another.

Champions are the people who recognize they have moved away from the Productivity Zone and can redirect themselves back quickly.

> ➤ *We are all human, so we will inevitably find ourselves in those other zones; the trick is to not live there.*

At my productivity bootcamp, we use football as a metaphor to explain the Productivity Zone. Your objective is the ball, and the optimal Productivity Zone is between the goal posts. To get the extra point, you don't need that ball to sail through the dead center of those posts, it just has to go through. Your score is the same no matter if the ball flies cleanly between the posts or bounces off one of them. So give yourself that flexibility and don't focus on, or become overwhelmed by, the idea of being in one fixed place within the Productivity Zone.

What Is Productivity?

Success and profits in your business are a result of productivity. It has nothing to do with time, and it has little to do with the state of the economy, although some business owners like to blame their failures on the prevailing business climate or lack of time. Blame lives on the outer edges of the productivity curve and is a sure fire way to keep you out of the Zone. You have to take personal responsibility to get in the zone by being positive, solution oriented, and ready for action.

Feel Productive

Productivity and success are mindsets. If you feel productive, or successful, then you are. If you feel busy and overwhelmed, you won't find success. Are you productive if you're always busy but aren't able to make time for your primary relationships? Are you productive if you're making money but are so tired and burned out that you don't enjoy it? What makes you feel productive and why? I have been criticized for this statement, but I think productivity is something that you feel, not something that you do.

> *Productivity is a feeling and personal assessment.*

Productivity=Profits

How do you know when you are in the Productivity Zone? When you experience the profits! Your level of productivity determines your profits. Keep in mind "profit" does not just mean "making money." If you spend one hundred thousand dollars to make fifty thousand dollars, did you profit? Obviously not! If you're at the overachiever end of the curve, chances are that you'll make money, but you probably won't maximize your profits. The difference is being in the Productivity Zone.

It's as simple as that! What I call "profit" actually appears in many forms: health, effective relationships (both at work and at home), joy, gratitude, peace of mind, passion, drive, ambition, and, of course, financial wealth. To me, profits are the natural byproduct of productivity.

The Inner Workings

Imagine that your total potential is like a windmill, abundant with limitless potential and natural resources, creating amazing momentum when everything is in sync. The windmill has a gear mechanism that works from within: The more smoothly, consistently, and quickly the blades turn, the more productive you tend to be.

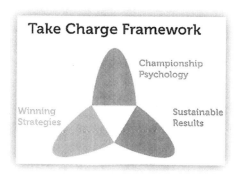

In taking charge of your productivity, there are three segments—or in windmill terminology, "blades"—that are critical. They are Championship Psychology, Winning Strategy and Sustainable Results. Without all three, your "productivity windmill" is underpowered. Yes, it might still turn, but not optimally.

Overall, there are 10 Core Drivers that make up these three blades:

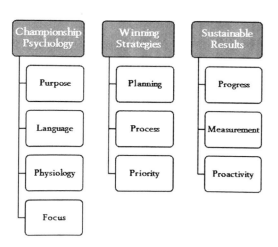

There's a sequence to success. These three sections, containing the subsets, need to be worked through in that order so that you can effectively and efficiently power your windmill.

The Time to Change Is NOW.

Maybe you've been where I was. Maybe you've seen your personal relationships suffer because of problems at work, or feared that you would lose your house, or wondered if your business could afford to stay open. Perhaps you've had sleepless nights worrying that you wouldn't be able to cover the bills this month, or felt guilty that you couldn't buy a holiday gift for your child.

Do you feel guilty because you missed important family events, like a birthday party or recital, because you couldn't afford to leave work? Are you angry and frustrated, or feel that you're not in control of your life, and desperately wish you just had **MORE TIME?**

You Are Not Alone

Most of my clients have been there. Nearly all business leaders wish they had more time. Once you commit to the 10 Core Drivers, you never have to feel that way, at least not for any extended period of time. The goal is to recognize uncomfortable emotions as a warning that your needs are not being met. You need to know how to read them, and then how to shift them as quickly as possible. That is what this book and my program are about because when you master these 10 Core Drivers, that doesn't just become possible, it becomes natural.

So congratulations on taking the first step. You are among the few who know you have a choice. By educating yourself on the 10 Core Drivers, you can take charge of your productivity, stop the procrastination and perfectionism, and start to use your time and energy in a more effective way. You'll get better results than you've ever had, and you'll accelerate your success.

TAKE AWAYS:

1. Take charge of your results to possess a full understanding of the factors that affect those desired outcomes.

2. There are 10 Core Drivers of productivity that help bring you to the Productivity Zone, and stay once you've arrived there: Purpose, Language, Physiology, Focus, Planning, Process, Priority, Progress, Measurement and Proactivity.

3. These 10 Core Drivers will provide you with achievement, flexibility, balance, and greater fulfillment—all found in the Productivity Zone.

CHAPTER 2: CHAMPIONSHIP PSYCHOLOGY

"Is time holding you back?"

"Success is 80% psychology and 20% mechanics"
- Tony Robbins

I WOKE UP LATE, MY hair was wet from a rushed shower, and I was desperate to get out the door. Ethan, my four-year-old son, was watching me as I frantically looked for my palm-pilot. I was mumbling to myself as I sometimes do. "I always have that in this top drawer," I grumbled as I checked there for the third time and grunted in disgust that it wasn't there. (Was it Einstein who said that the definition of insanity is doing the same thing over and over again and expecting a different result?)

Ethan chimed in and said, "Lisa never puts things back in the right places."

This stopped me in my tracks. It was horrifying to hear my four-year old son blaming our housekeeper. Blaming sounds so ugly, and worst of all, I knew he must have been mimicking me. I turned to my son and told him "Lisa helps us to straighten the house, and if we don't put things back where they should go, then she does her best to tidy things up. It is up to us to put it away properly. I have to take responsibility for that."

My son's awful words resonated in my ears and filled my thoughts all day. It was a rude awakening. I was letting myself fall into a destructive pattern of blaming. That time it was over something small, but it made me wonder where else was that showing up that I wasn't aware of? Passing the buck in any form is not who I am. It will not bring me greater success. I realized I must change that behavior, especially after seeing how it was poisoning my son's mind.

———◆———

➤ *You have to identify the virus before you can treat it.*

Our psychology and mindset are the driving forces behind everything that we do, and as a result, everything that we accomplish. Scientists and champion athletes alike have learned that mastering anything is ninety-five percent psychology and five percent skills.

Ultimately, Championship Psychology isn't just a blade in that productivity windmill we discussed in the first chapter; it's the foundation, gears, and even the wind. Without a solid foundation, well-oiled gears, and wind blowing in the right direction, you won't generate or harness your power.

To better understand what it takes to create a Championship Psychology, let's break it down.

Here are the four key elements that form **Championship Psychology**:

1. PURPOSE

2. LANGUAGE

3. PHYSIOLOGY

4. FOCUS

We'll explore these in depth in later chapters, but for now, let's talk about Championship Psychology as a whole. Let's start with understanding what it takes to be a champion.

In my experience, many people think champion behavior is innate, an aspect of personality that one is simply born with. For example, if your father was a champion, naturally you'll be one, too. And if not, you're doomed. The good news is there is no champion gene. Of course, it seems easy to say there is a champion gene and you didn't get it. Or, that it is easy for someone else to make great achievements because they have it. But being a champion isn't easy for anyone. It requires desire, dedication, commitment, perseverance, and practice. Champions are not born; they are made.

I didn't wake up one day with a sudden insight into what makes some people wildly successful where others have failed. These 10 Core Drivers didn't come to me in a dream; they are the result of years of investment, research, effort, and resources.

➢ *Being a champion is a state of being that you create.*

Your state of mind may change with the circumstances, but champions bring their best even when the chips are down. As a result, they shift quickly and LET GO of a negative emotion/mood to overcome obstacles and find their way back to that positive mindset and driving force.

It Isn't about Time

First, I'm going to let you in on my biggest secret: Success has nothing (and I do mean NOTHING) to do with **time**. Time Management is the greatest challenge that most of my clients report, but it has little effect on their productivity and/or profits! Time is a constant. You can't control it, and you can't make more of it. Time doesn't fly or run out. We can't create it, but it is a precious commodity.

In order to understand how to consistently achieve what we want with the least amount of effort, we need to go to the root cause of the challenge, the main driver.

➤ *What really matters is energy.*

You can spend all day on a project, you can devote months or even years. But if you aren't bringing your best energy to it, you won't get the best results. What you can change is how much of yourself you are bringing to the time you have, and how you feel about the results you create. The first blade of the windmill is focused on this point. It's called Championship Psychology. It allows you to be in control of your mood, attitude, and energy. Once you shift your perspective away from time and towards energy you'll start seeing better results almost immediately.

➤ *Championship Psychology is how we manage our energy!*

Presuppositions of a Championship Psychology

There are 7 Principles that support a Champion. Champions don't just say these. They aren't mantras. Rather they are states of being:

1. You create your own identity

2. Choice is your greatest gift

3. Energy is everything

4. Ask quality questions

5. What is learned can be unlearned

6. No failure, only feedback

7. Environment is paramount

As you progress through the chapters on Championship Psychology, keep these 7 presuppositions—or principles—in mind. What would change about the way you live your life if you approached your challenges with the 7 Principles?

Just When You Think All Is Well . . .

I was living a dream life in Switzerland with my adventurous and handsome husband, Robert. We were always jetting off to some adventure or another, whether it was a lengthy geo-hunt, racing our tandem mountain bikes, or camping in the Swiss Mountains. We were never bored. After a few years, we were blessed with a son, and then shortly after that, a daughter. We lived in a beautiful house, and both of us had successful careers that afforded us many luxuries, such as a nanny, a ski chalet, and frequent family vacations. At that point, my life was going exactly according to plan. It was easy to wake up each morning feeling like a champion.

After fifteen years together, with no measurable warning, on his birthday, Robert announced to me that he was unhappy and that he didn't love me anymore. All at once that dream life came crashing down. I was crushed. I had thought our lives were as near to perfect as lives could be. What could there be to improve on? I didn't nag, our sex life was still very active, we stayed fit and healthy together, our house was clean, and there was plenty of money. WHAT was there to be unhappy about?

My heart ached. How do you stop loving? I asked him if there was someone else, and he swore there wasn't. Spoiler Alert: He'd been having an affair for several months. I didn't find out about his affair until much later, though I suspected there was someone else. But during those first few months after he gave me the "I don't love you anymore" speech, I was convinced we could "fix this." We could become even closer. What can I say? I am an eternal optimist.

How does one cope in these highly stressful situations? Where was I finding this optimism? I didn't realize it at the time, but I asked myself some key questions that helped me cope and stay calm. First I asked, "What could this mean?" Was he going through a midlife crisis? Were his needs not getting met in the relationship? Was he not getting enough sleep? (We still had challenges with our youngest, who at one year old, was not yet sleeping through the night.) I needed to clearly review my part in this and own it. I did my soul searching, and it helped me to see things from his perspective and identify what I needed to learn and change. I worked hard to show him I loved him, but I could only do my part. After a good six months, I could see he wasn't willing to meet me half-way; he wasn't willing to ask himself the same questions I had. The relationship, as much as I wanted to keep it alive, needed the effort and cooperation of us both.

Champions Focus on the Goals and Purpose

In those first months after Robert told me he didn't love me, I learned how hard it is to be a champion when the chips are down. My family and friends wanted to tar and feather him, and suggested I throw all his things out on the front lawn. Those were the nicer of the suggestions. Although it was tempting, and might have felt good for a quick minute, what would that have solved? It was suggested I keep a journal of the wrongs Robert had done me—his personal criminal record. But how could that help me heal or correct the course that Robert and I were on?

Instead, I did the opposite. I focused on what I was grateful for even though some days it was hard to tune in to that frequency. Deep down I knew my life would turn out the way it was meant to and that this would somehow be to my benefit. I thought, "This too shall pass."

I believe everything happens for a reason, even if we don't know what it is. This belief has always given me comfort to fall back on when I've had no control over the situation. I gave my full effort, with all my heart and soul, to reconcile with my husband and show up at my best for both him and my children. It wasn't easy, but I created an environment and habits that enabled me to do that. As difficult as it was, after a set period of time (I gave it six months), I accepted that we were not meant to be together.

Choose Your Story

There's more to the story, but for now I will just say I have no regrets about our life together. I constantly focus on the good things our relationship produced. Not only do I have two amazing children, I traveled around Europe and stretched my comfort zone athletically by doing mountain marathons, glacier walking, and scuba diving. On the business front, I built a successful multimillion dollar business, among other accomplishments. Robert was a great mentor to me and influenced much of that. All my experiences have influenced my growth and development in a positive way. That is the story I continue to tell myself. It's much healthier than recalling the hurt and pain. Both stories are true, absolutely, but I control the story I choose to live in.

I am proud of how I handled the split up and the divorce. I didn't know it at the time, but the keys to my growth, amicable divorce, and current friendly relationship with Robert were due to the four Core Drivers of Championship Psychology.

After a few years, I re-evaluated our situation, his involvement (or lack thereof), what I really wanted, and what was best for the kids. I made the choice to return with my children to the United States to be closer to my family and start another company. Although there was a great deal of challenge, change, and uncertainty, I am now living my life with greater passion and purpose than I ever had before. I wouldn't wish my experience on anyone, but I am stronger AND happier for it.

Why am I sharing this intimate story with you? Because I want you to understand through my experience that being a champion isn't all sunshine and roses. To get where you want to go, you'll need true grit. There is challenge and resistance, courage and commitment. Being a champion means bringing the best of you, especially when it is difficult to do. I chose to face the truth with integrity and gratitude, and I was able to meet the challenge. And that was a gift. After all, if we aren't challenged, we'll never know what we're capable of. Sometimes being a champion is staying true to who you are and who you want to be, even when everything else is crumbling.

"It is not the strongest or the most intelligent who will survive but those who can best manage change."

— Charles Darwin

Even though my marriage did not succeed, I still treated Robert and myself with respect throughout the separation process. No matter the magnitude of emotion I felt around the challenge, I did my best to handle the situation as a champion. And I am proud to say that today as a result, I have an easy relationship with my former husband. My children thrive despite the divorce because their parents show respect to one another—which makes it easier on them and is conducive to their stability. In this case, my children are my purpose. My mental focus drives my self-talk and the language I choose to use, which has a direct impact on my outcome.

➤ *Manage your thoughts, feelings, and triggers, not the clock.*

Do you think Steve Jobs, Apple's Founder, worried about whether it took an extra hour here and there while he was developing the iPod? Do you think Michael Phelps, the most decorated Olympian of all time, ever allowed himself to believe he didn't have time to swim today? Do you think Michael Jordan ever looked at his practice schedule and said, "Where will I find the time?" I doubt it. You can't create time, and you can't lose it either. Instead, think of time as a structure to help you focus and stay on a purpose driven path. A game is no fun and cannot be played without rules and boundaries. In the game of life, time is a boundary.

To sum it all up, if you're allowing yourself to wallow in unproductive self-talk, or if you're focusing on the wrong priorities and goals, or if you're not taking care of yourself, you're wasting time and draining your future energy reserves. Once you tap into your championship psychology, time management will become a non-issue. It's how you manage your energy that will allow you to stay at the peak of the productivity curve and get the results you seek.

Take Aways:

1. Purpose, Language, Physiology, and Focus affect every aspect of our lives and determine our outcomes. Incorporating these elements, along with the 7 Principles of a Championship Psychology will allow you to overcome any obstacle.

2. You choose your reality by the story you create for yourself.

3. Championship Psychology is about managing energy, not time.

CHAPTER 3: PURPOSE

WAIT FOR IT   WATCH IT SOAR

"See things as you would have them be instead of how they are."

- Robert Collier

LADIES AND GENTLEMEN, START YOUR . . . BIKES!!!
I was standing in a crowd of mountain bike racers, eager to begin a fifty-mile mountain bike half-marathon in the Swiss Alps. I was in the best shape of my life. I'd trained for weeks! But the obstacles ahead were staggering. I'd be facing a ten thousand-foot overall ascent across three mountain peaks, and mind you, this was only HALF of the full race.

The climb began almost immediately and didn't stop for what felt like an eternity. My butt clenched in the seat, I powered up for all I was worth when, suddenly, I was having excruciating pains in muscles I didn't even know I had. I had been an avid mountain biker for years, but I had never experienced pain like this before. I didn't know how I was going to pedal one more foot, let alone make it to the finish line. I needed to get off the bike—that instant! Fortunately, as we rounded the corner, there was a traffic jam where the trail merged to a single track into the woods. I dismounted the tandem bike I was riding with my husband and noticed that my adrenalin had died down a bit. It was not far into the race, but I really didn't think I could continue. The idea of stopping here was unbearable, but so was the pain that I'd be experiencing once we started back up. I didn't think I could handle it. Luckily, we were queued up waiting our entry into the woods for thirty minutes or so, and I had a little bit of physical recovery time, as well as the time I needed to get emotionally centered. I laid out a psychological plan. I decided I could do this and focused on one step at a time. I knew that if I could break down the daunting challenges into individual pieces, I could handle each one rather than having to tackle the whole. Soon, I was stoking up my confidence level, and before I even realized it, I was back on the bike, and the pain was gone.

Then, another hour into the ride, we came to a very steep single track where we actually had to carry our bike! That's when I realized that whoever designed this race was a total sadist. I pictured him or her above us in a helicopter, looking down with binoculars and laughing at our struggles. Who designs a bike race where you have to carry your frikin' bike?!

And then I got mad and tapped into an energy reserve I didn't know existed. My anger became a source of motivation—an emotional fuel. I said to myself, "I'm going to finish this race if it kills me." It practically did a few times as a result of the speed on some of those steep hills.

Now, the thing about a two-seater mountain bike is that it's heavy, so it develops serious momentum going down those hills.

Because this was a big race with lots of racers, I was imagining a worst-case scenario. I was scared we would crash and someone would get hurt. I pictured a huge pile-up with significant injuries to any rider in our path .The next thing I knew, I was screaming at the top of my lungs. "Move! You have to move! Get out of the way!" We couldn't slow down, and were hurtling down the course at a reckless speed. To say it was dangerous was an understatement.

All in all, it was seven hours biking on the most demanding terrain I have ever experienced. I had never done anything nearly as challenging as that before in my life. But even with my backside killing me, tears of joy, accomplishment, and pride welled up as I crossed that finish line.

This was a moment I would never forget. This was as hard as it gets and I was doing it. It made me aware of how much I am really capable of; how much we are *all* capable of.

➢ *Pushing your comfort zone is the only way you achieve what you are truly capable of.*

———◆———

That bike race became one of those experiences that shaped my identity. I knew that I could overcome any challenge or obstacle and it made me realize that I can perform beyond what I thought my limits were.

➢ *Having a clear purpose defines and refines you, either in its fulfillment or in its pursuit.*

Having a clear goal and purpose is an essential part of Championship Psychology and an integral part of what motivates you and drives your productivity. Purpose is what gets you up in the morning to do whatever it is you do and makes your hard work, time, and energy worthwhile. That clear purpose creates perseverance and enables you to overcome challenges as they arise. It puts you in control, creates focus, and even kills procrastination. With purpose, you gain the clarity to set priorities, tap desire, and find the willpower and commitment to achieve your goals. A clear purpose fuels the creativity that helps you get things done faster and more effectively. This is true for you as an individual, and also for any organization.

When there is a lack of clarity, it creates scattered and arbitrary actions. Organizations suffer from political problems and undesirable competition, competing priorities, and a lack of drive for innovation and creativity. In contrast, when we look at many start-up organizations, hierarchies are flat, and people have a strong and clear purpose to do what it takes to reach the company goals. People work selflessly in collaboration. That is what clear purpose does for an organization.

In this chapter we'll look at WHAT the key components of Purpose are and HOW you go about tapping into it. This could be a discovery you make for the first time, or a chance to reconnect with the things that make you tick. Either way, connecting with it will supercharge your productivity.

Know and Connect with Your "WHY"

The first aspect of Purpose is WHY. Why are you pursuing something? What do you stand for? Why do you do what you do? To get to the core desire, ask yourself these questions. "When I achieve what I want to, how will I feel about that result?" "How will I feel about what I did to get there?" "How will I know I have achieved it?" "What will now be different?"

These may seem like simple questions to answer for some, yet profoundly daunting for others.

For most people, illuminating why you do what you do will be an "aha" moment where you suddenly realize you are (or maybe you aren't) headed toward the place you want to go. Connecting with your "Why" can have a transformational effect on your goals and dreams. It's also an important step to knowing and accepting who you really are, which can be incredibly grounding. That's what we mean when we say our purpose "refines and defines" who we are and how we see ourselves. It gives our lives meaning and significance, helping us grow into more of who we are and who we want to be.

For some of you, it has been a while since you connected with your "Why." Unconsciously, your focus has scattered, and you have become disconnected. It is time to get reconnected.

> *Connecting with why you want something can make all the difference in achieving it.*

Pick Your Path

Just prior to my husband's announcement that he didn't love me anymore, I was in line to be CEO of the Swiss office for GFK, the fourth largest market research company in the world. My boss had brought me on to be the member of the executive team responsible for strategic projects. After only one year, he then asked me to take over a failing division that I had been working to turnaround. And shortly after that, I realized I was being groomed to take his position after he retired. I thought this might be conjecture on my part, until he told me flat out that he wanted me to succeed him. Me!

Since I was the newest member of the executive team, an American, and a woman (the Swiss were still a bit chauvinistic),

I was surprised to say the least. I was also tremendously flattered—excited by the idea and all the significance the position held. This was way beyond the corner office and all the perks of my initial success.

Know What's Right for You

Yet there was also this nagging discomfort that I didn't understand. Was it fear of a position of this magnitude? Did I question if I could do it? Yes, of course there was a little of that . . . but then one day it hit me: I didn't want this position. The dream job wasn't right for me despite the fact that others thought it was and that I had the skills to do it. I realized the position wasn't what I wanted. My boss was like a father figure to me, and I wanted to please him—but not at the expense of not walking my own path.

The feedback I was getting from everyone, even my husband, was that this job was perfect for me, tailored to suit me. What could I possibly be thinking by turning it down, thereby losing my job altogether? Surely I had lost my mind. A coveted position like this didn't present itself every day.

But I had started to evaluate (for the first time really) what I stood for, what I was working towards, and why I wanted it. My career had just developed into this. Come to think of it, I had no real direction up to this point. That is what happens when we have no real goals or purpose: our lives just develop and not always in the direction we want, so we settle for what comes easily. I hadn't guided my own arrow. When I spent time thinking about what I really enjoyed and felt passionate about, I saw clearly that my gift was in developing strategies and people, client and team engagement, and finding and breaking through challenges. Also I took a good look at my children's ages and what kind of mom I wanted to be. Like it or not, being the CEO of a major corporation was not the best way for me to serve those passions.

I always knew I wanted to have an impact on the world, and even though I wasn't sure what that might look like, I knew this wasn't it. So to the astonishment of everyone around me, I took what I considered to be a courageous step and declined that role.

This was happening at the same time my marriage was falling apart, and the timing could not have been worse. Crazy as it may seem, with all of this going on, I knew I would be fine. It was like I was in the eye of the storm, with chaos all around me, but I found clarity and a sense of calm within myself.

◆

You'll Know It When You Feel It

I didn't know where my path would take me, but I was now following it. I had been working with a coach and had started a path of self-development/discovery. I loved getting to know myself better, and I loved coaching. I had always enjoyed making things better and using technology as a vehicle. I discovered the greatest leverage to make things better was by improving ourselves, not the technology. I knew relatively quickly that coaching was what I wanted to do. I wanted to help people resolve their core challenges and grow their businesses to get to the next level of their development. Because of my own successes and failures, I was able to coach at the highest level by combining business skills and a winning mindset.

About eighteen months later, after I completed my coaching certification and after some soul searching, I knew that it was time to return to the U.S. The sixteen years I had spent in Switzerland had been an important part of my personal development, but after all the changes in my life, I felt like it was time to begin a new chapter back in the USA. Leaving a well-paid job and moving my children, now three and five, to another country was no small step, but my purpose was clearer and it gave me the courage to get outside of my comfort zone to achieve it, whatever "*it*" was exactly.

I called my return to the United States "rediscovering the American culture." The time I spent away allowed me to see my native country with a fresh perspective. I knew intuitively that the underlying purpose had something to do with culture, but I still wasn't sure what or how. Shortly after arriving back in the U.S., I started a project to create a blog platform to influence greater cultural awareness by engaging people to write about their cultural experiences. The idea was to introduce the underlying theme of personal responsibility for our cultural development. But a few months into this project, I realized I was delegating most of the work. Obviously this was not lighting me up. If it had, I wouldn't have been able to put it down. That was the case in my software development projects and my private client coaching sessions. My passion, I was learning, lived in helping others overcome obstacles to make their businesses more successful and in transforming the way they think and do things to achieve a Championship Psychology. That's what really turned me on, got me out of bed, and fired up my day. This was . . . this is . . . my purpose in life.

Knowing what you want is important, and understanding why you want it, adds more passion and depth. By connecting to your WHY, you are aligning your heart and your head. This will give you the desire, determination, and commitment you need to stay the course, especially when you have to do mundane or less interesting tasks that are part of making it happen. Creating a vision is easy; doing what it takes and reaching your goals is the part that takes courage, action, and perseverance.

Your Purpose Extends Beyond You

Going through my divorce was not easy, but my purpose during the process was clear: My children, unquestionably, were the most important element in the equation, and I did not want them put in the middle in any way. I did everything possible to reconcile with their father and make the best decisions I could for their sake. Not trashing my ex wasn't easy as the story about his affair unfolded. But by showing respect to their father, my children felt safe in loving each of us and, in turn, felt secure in our love for them.

Even though my emotions were high at times, I came back to my WHY, and though that didn't make it easy, it put things in perspective and allowed me to let go of other things that got in the way.

You Can Let Go

In order to really let go, you have to first decide to let go. Sounds simple but often we don't decide because we aren't ready. If you aren't sure you can let go, think about the true consequences of these actions both short and long term. The consequences can be to your emotional state, health, finances, and relationships—all of which have a profound effect on your time and energy. Then, think about all the people around you who are affected. How might these emotional actions cost you the very thing you really wanted? Is it really worth it?

> ➢ *When you have a strong WHY, you will find the courage to let go.*

On occasion the kids, their dad and I will go out and do things together. We chose to make things easy. When your purpose extends beyond yourself, it makes those choices obvious. I take the same approach in my business when expectations aren't met in a business deal or project. It is easy to be taken away by our emotions, but by staying focused on the purpose, goal, or objective you can avoid poor decisions and a lot of conflict.

Connecting and Reconnecting to Your WHY: A Case Study

One of my best friends is a doctor in Washington. He's incredibly passionate about his work, and he takes enormous pride in helping others heal their bodies and minds. Like most people, he is NOT passionate about paperwork. When he left the army to pursue medicine, he envisioned himself working holistically with patients, learning about their lives, and setting them on a path to healthy living. What he did not envision were the hours spent in front of a computer or on hold with insurance companies. After about ten years in practice, he found himself putting off paperwork, not getting it done on time (or at all!), and resenting each second he spent on it. He came to me for coaching, feeling unhappy in his chosen pursuit.

I worked with him on connecting to his WHY. His purpose, after all, was to heal, and without correctly processed paperwork and insurance filings, his patients wouldn't be able to see him. To keep his motivation front and center before him, I suggested that he get a picture of each patient, an easy task as most of them had a picture ID copied into their files. I then had him put that picture where he could see it while working on that patient's paperwork. Any time he began to feel resentful of his "wasted time," he was to look at the picture and think of that patient's challenges and what they would need to heal.

Soon he found that he was able to view the paperwork as an extension of each individual, rather than as something that was being forced upon him. In less than six weeks, he went from being tragically behind on his documentation to having it done at the end of every single workday. Without needing to set a whole day aside to catch up on paperwork from the week before, he was able to begin working only four days a week. He now spends a three-day weekend with his family each and every week! Connecting to his WHY during the mundane tasks has allowed him to transform how he lives his life.

───◆───

Own Your WHY

I suspect this concept isn't new to you, but here is the part you may not know: There's more to finding your purpose than just knowing your WHY. You have to **own** your WHY. That is what makes it stick and keeps it sustainable.

Here are three components to owning your WHY:

1. **GROWTH**

2. **SELF-DEFINITION OR IDENTITY**

3. **CONTRIBUTION**

These three musketeers of purpose are about understanding not just who you are now, but who you want to be and what you want to bring to the world. Growth is how we discover our WHY, identity locks it in so we own it, and contribution is how we share it! After all, you can't find your WHY if you haven't found yourself. It's a common theme in literature and film for people to be stuck in the process of finding themselves.

What do you want to be when you grow up? Some of us know the answer early on. For others, it can take years of self-investigation. And some of us who know don't seem to be able to make it off the launching pad. How do we start? And, if we've taken those early steps, how do we rise to the dreams we keep in our hearts? This is why "coming of age" stories are so popular. They speak to the human condition. Whether we know it or not, we're constantly on a quest to define and accept ourselves.

GROWTH

The First Part of Owning Your WHY

Growth comes from learning something positive and applying it to your life, creating a higher level of achievement, and more importantly, fulfillment and satisfaction. I challenge you to not feel satisfied and fulfilled when you've experienced personal growth. Actually, I dare you! It is impossible. Physiologically, you can't help but feel good when you've grown. That's because it's a chemical reaction, literally. Our brains release dopamine and serotonin, reinforcing the behavior that helped you grow. It's not a stretch to say that growth is addictive, but in the most positive way.

Growth can result from either large or small events, slowly pulling at you until you are ready to take the steps needed to embrace who you want to become or who you really are.

My marriage, for example, may have ended, but I learned a lot about myself and how I communicate. The experience shook me to the core of my being and left me off-kilter, but it did have many positive side benefits. I had to regain my self-confidence and define myself anew. In this process, I became stronger and more assured at a deeper level.

In order to grow, you have to be challenged and learn something from the experience. Challenges stretch our comfort zones and may even redefine the way we think of others and ourselves. Dramatic growth occurs when we face and overcome an obstacle, learn from the event, and create a positive meaning we can share with others.

I call this the Rubber Band Effect, because the more we're challenged and stretched, the more tension it creates, and the farther we will snap and grow when released. It's the force tugging us against our will, and our force responding to it, that create the internal expansion.

My father's sudden death when I was nineteen, my divorce, the birth of my children, my move to Switzerland at age twenty-five, my return to the U.S. after sixteen years, and the emotional circumstances surrounding these events stretched my comfort zones. You have had your emotional events too, and with each life-altering event, your abilities and potential have stretched and grown, whether you were aware of it or not.

———◆———

➤ *Growth doesn't occur until we find the lessons within the challenges.*

Like a character in a book embarking on a quest of self-discovery, be grateful for what you have and the lessons you've learned. As Mother Theresa famously said, "I know the Lord won't give me more than I can handle. I just wish He didn't trust me so much." Whatever it is that's stretching your rubber band, take comfort in knowing it won't stretch beyond what you're capable of . . . because you're capable of infinite stretching! With each new experience, you will develop an even greater capacity. Instead, crazy as it seems, try to welcome and accept the challenges and see them as opportunities to grow. First, you will get through them faster and easier than if you fight them. Second, they're going to happen anyway, so why not choose to accept or welcome them? How you interpret them is your choice.

"Pain is inevitable, but suffering is a choice"

\- Haruki Murakami

SELF-DEFINITION OR IDENTITY

Who Are You?

Your identity is the strongest force determining the results you get in your life. Despite the desire to grow or change, we'll usually remain true to our current definition of ourselves. So, stop and ask yourself: How do I define myself?

When I was in high school, like many teenagers, I started smoking. I suppose I thought it was cool. And all my friends were doing it. So stir in some peer pressure as to why I took on such a harmful habit. By the end of my freshman year in college, I was smoking a pack a day. Since my friends all smoked, it became part of our social interaction, and I really enjoyed it. But here's the surprise. When I thought about who I was and what I valued, I never really considered myself "a smoker;" it was just something I did. It was never a label I gave myself.

Then I started dating a guy who didn't smoke. I didn't want to smoke in front of him because he might consider it a disgusting, dirty habit. What if he wanted to kiss me and I had smoker's breath? One night he was at my apartment and we were having a great time. Then from nowhere, a deep and sudden urge to go out for a smoke hit me. I couldn't get my mind off it. The craving to smoke was stronger than my desire to be with him, a guy I really liked!

So, determined to get my nicotine fix, I fabricated a reason that he had to leave. After he was gone, and after I finished my cigarette, I realized how ridiculous that was! I understood the insanity of dismissing a guy I really wanted to spend time with JUST SO I COULD HAVE A CIGARETTE! And that was my last cigarette. I quit on the spot. Now, I won't pretend I didn't have physical cravings for nicotine after that, but studies have shown those go away after the nicotine is out of your system, which only took a few days. What's harder to break is the habit—the emotional connection with smoking. But because I didn't define myself as a smoker, it was easier to stop. I had a greater incentive not to do it.

I believe the reason most people struggle with giving up cigarettes, aside from the nicotine craving, is that they still identify themselves as smokers. They still see themselves as smokers deprived of smoking. When you spend your time counting the days that you haven't indulged in a behavior, you're still engaged, marking time, and probably keeping your options open. In short, you may not be planning to quit for good.

Subconsciously, you may be marking the days until your next cigarette. Sure, in the beginning you start counting to keep track and give yourself a boost. But in order to really change a habit, you must first change how you define yourself. This is true of any behavior that you want to add, remove, or change: If it's not a part of your self-definition, your change will only be temporary.

Choose Yourself and Your Self-definition

What determined who you are and how you approach your life? Was it your parents, your religious beliefs, the environment of your childhood, your financial situation? All of these are powerful influences, no doubt. So powerful that they can obscure the one truth that can change your life. How you define yourself is actually *your own choice*.

No matter how you got here, the beliefs and behaviors you've formed over time can be changed. What stands in the way for most people is that their sense of self is based on things they simply have "known" to be true. But it wasn't long ago that we KNEW the world was flat, or that the sun orbited the moon, or that man would never be able to fly. Our ancestors knew those as "facts," and they dictated how people dealt with the world and put unnecessary limitations on them and cultural development.

A belief is just something we are "certain" of due to our limited experiences, values, and past decisions. When we get new information and perspectives, we open up our ability to change and form new beliefs. You weren't born believing these things. For us to become our best selves, we'd be well served to choose more productive and inspiring beliefs.

I often work with companies frustrated with their sales performance. For example, I worked with a one hundred million dollar company that felt its sales people weren't reaching their potential because the company seemed to hit a plateau it couldn't rise above. Psychologists call this a "glass ceiling," a self-created barrier resulting from a person's limited self-definition. It was clear to my client why certain salespeople wouldn't take on accounts over a certain size. The sales people didn't see themselves as five million dollar producers, so unconsciously they sabotaged their own efforts to keep their identity intact. This happens to business owners, too, with reaching the one million dollar and five million dollar revenue mark.

"Our behavior will be consistent with our self-definition"
- Maxwell Malz.

The good news is that once the ceiling is broken, we can repeat our successes. For example, what happened when Roger Banister broke the four-minute mile? Other runners stepped up and followed suit. Why? Because the beliefs and thinking that held them back before, this idea that they "couldn't do it," had been replaced with proof that it could be done! Once that becomes part of the sales person's identity, watch out! In this case, one of the sales people attracted and closed a million dollar deal after our workshop—and removed the glass ceiling. He is on his way to being a five million dollar producer who will no longer get in his own way.

What Defines You Today?

The first step in creating your ideal identity is recognizing how you define yourself now. I'm betting you've never really given it much thought, so this will be new for you. It will open up a whole new awareness of how you define yourself.

Take a sheet of paper and write down "I am _____"
fifty times down the whole page. Repeatedly ask yourself, "Who
am I? What are my core beliefs? What drives me? What are my
'deal-breakers'?" The answers comprise your current self-
definition, as you see yourself today.

Now review your answers. Can you see the limitations that
accompany your definition? What do you notice about the
language you used? Have you defined yourself by your
profession? There is so much more to you than that! Here is a
startling fact: sixteen percent of people die within five years of
retirement, and the study that yielded these results used a
retirement age of sixty-five! That's what can happen when your
profession defines your identity. When your profession is gone,
unconsciously you feel like you don't have value, and you stop
growing. The same is true if your relationship defines you: "I am
Mrs. So-and-so." When that relationship ceases to exist—
through death, divorce, or separation—people feel lost and have
a hard time moving on with their lives.

The Road to a New You

Describe who you want to become. Write it down in vivid
detail. See it, feel it, hear it—like a song in your mind's ear. In
order to live at that level, what beliefs do you need to have?
What rituals and habits would you have to adopt? What
environment do you need to be a part of? What type of friends
and acquaintances will be the best fit for that new you?

The following diagram illustrates the steps you'll follow in
creating or changing your self-definition.

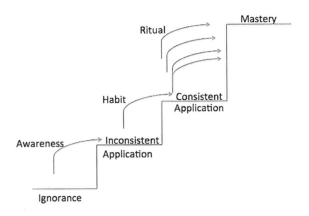

1.   CREATE AWARENESS

2.   MAKE IT A HABIT

3.   LOCK IT IN AS A RITUAL

1. CREATE AWARENESS

Awareness is the first step.
Awareness is always the first step to changing. You have to be keenly mindful of the habit or behavior you want to change. At this stage, you may not know anything else, such as why you're behaving that way, how deeply ingrained the behavior may be, or the path to change. And that's fine. The goal is simply admit something has got to give and begin to understand more about yourself in relation to your behavior. You're beginning to acquire the skills and knowledge needed for creating a change. When I asked my potential boy friend to leave, my awareness broke through, which triggered a desire to quit smoking. The new awareness was my personal alert that it was time to do something.

2. MAKE IT A HABIT

Habits vs. Rituals

Step two is making yourself aware of the triggers that usually lead to the behavior you're trying to change, and then researching and implementing ways to stop. At this stage, it's common to make some progress in fits and starts. Your application is inconsistent or not sustainable. It still requires a great deal of effort and may have you wondering if you can change at all. The good news is that this is normal. Step three is where the magic happens.

3. LOCK IT IN AS A RITUAL

In this stage, you commit, and you reevaluate your self-definition to make this change a "must." When a habit becomes a ritual, it is part of your self-definition. Ultimately, this means what once required more thought and energy to maintain is now automatic. If you decide that you are an Olympic swimmer like Michael Phelps, then waking up every morning to practice is a must. This will happen every day, regardless of the amount of sleep you had, the weather conditions, or if you're on vacation. You train because that's who you are.

Understand that when you're inconsistently applying a corrective behavior, it falls under the category of something you "should do." But when it's part of who you are and how you define yourself, it becomes a "must do." In my smoking story, what enabled me to quit cold turkey was that *I did not want to define myself as a smoker*. I became aware that this behavior was holding me back from what I really wanted and was incongruent with who I was. The message to myself wasn't "I should not smoke any more" but rather "I must not smoke. This isn't who I am."

> ➤ *Rituals occur when they are a part of your self-definition, and therefore make the action a must.*

Manage Your Environment

"Diaries are kept by men: strong brushstrokes on smooth mulberry paper, gathered into sheaves and tied with ribbon and placed in a lacquered box."
- THE FOX WOMAN, Kij Johnson

"Everything starts somewhere, although many physicists disagree."
- HOGFATHER, Terry Pratchett

"Taran wanted to make a sword; but Coll, charged with the practical side of his education, decided on horseshoes."
-THE BOOK OF THREE, Lloyd Alexander

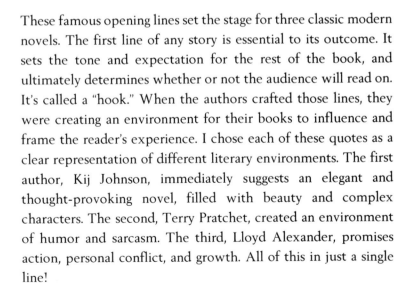

These famous opening lines set the stage for three classic modern novels. The first line of any story is essential to its outcome. It sets the tone and expectation for the rest of the book, and ultimately determines whether or not the audience will read on. It's called a "hook." When the authors crafted those lines, they were creating an environment for their books to influence and frame the reader's experience. I chose each of these quotes as a clear representation of different literary environments. The first author, Kij Johnson, immediately suggests an elegant and thought-provoking novel, filled with beauty and complex characters. The second, Terry Pratchet, created an environment of humor and sarcasm. The third, Lloyd Alexander, promises action, personal conflict, and growth. All of this in just a single line!

Now consider how much environment can impact your story! Just as these authors set the stage for their characters, you need to set the stage for your life, and that means managing your environment.

Environment Is Paramount

Environment can make or break your success. In the shift from habits to rituals, how you manage your environment plays a critical role. Consider an Olympic athlete. They eat, drink and breathe their sport. They create schedules and plan meals to support their preparation and practice. They live in group housing with others who have the same passion to be their best. And they have coaches and sponsors to hold them accountable and push them to their limits.

Environments can create success, but they can also cause contamination. Why do forty to sixty percent of drug addicts return to using drugs after coming out of rehab? (AMA, 2000) Partly it's due to their friendships because their friends are users. But it's also the old, familiar places. The momentarily reformed addict goes back home and is subjected to the same negative emotional triggers that are linked to the original destructive behavior.

Consider the people, places, and things you surround yourself with and the influence they have on your self-definition.

Choose Your Friends Wisely

"Show me your friends and I'll show you your future."
                                    - Chaplain Ronnie Melancon

Our friends don't define us, but they do reflect us. By choosing to surround yourself with people who love you, support you, and challenge you to grow, you create an environment that is predisposed to productivity. Think of friends and colleagues as an investment in your future.

I've invested wisely in myself by joining some mastermind groups that put me in the same company as famous actors, successful business leaders, and successful experts in their fields. These environments have allowed me to stretch and expand my intellect, my perspective, my network, and most importantly, my heart. Some of my dearest friends have come from these groups. They've held me to a higher standard.

Conversely, if you're in a "toxic" relationship, romantic or otherwise, it will impact your self-definition, your self-confidence, and your self-worth. Your game will suffer. People are with us for "a reason, a season, or a lifetime." Don't be afraid to walk away from people who are holding you down, holding you back, or even just holding you still. Appreciate the reason or season they have been in your life and how they have enriched your life, and then move on to those who are better suited for your development. We will discuss this further in the next chapter, but for now, consider the relationships you have: personal, romantic, and professional. How many of these truly support you, challenge you, and inspire you to push for even greater results?

CONTRIBUTION

All the lessons learned along the way are what make up your unique experience and contribute to your self-expression.

> ➤ *The expression and application of growth becomes*
>   *your value and contribution.*

Share and Add Value

Contribution means finding the value you bring to the world and sharing it. Most people will do more for other people than they will do for themselves. Contribution is a powerful motivator and part of our purpose. What value have you created today? What value do you want to create in the future? For what contribution do you want to be remembered? How did you make a difference, and for whom?

I had a client who had a deep desire to contribute to women, animals, and veterans. He had a big heart. He envisioned creating a multi-million dollar foundation to serve others. When he talked about his vision, it was powerful beyond measure. He realized the foundation would be a huge undertaking that would take time, but in the meanwhile he identified that he could start contributing in the here and now by becoming a Big Brother. I was confused when he hadn't taken action by our next session. As it turned out, it was his own insecurity and lack of appreciation of his personal value that held him back from being there for others.

At a PTA meeting a few nights before, I had heard the starfish story and shared it with him. The story goes like this: There were miles of starfish washed up onto the shore. Without water, they were bound to die. A young man walking the beach began throwing the starfish back into the water one at a time. Another man came up and asked him what he was doing, arguing there was no way to make a difference with the miles of starfish on the shore. The first young man picked up another starfish and threw it into the water saying, "Maybe, but it made a difference for that one." Hearing this story, combined with overcoming his limiting emotional obstacles, my client was inspired to take action and contribute in whatever way he could. He knew everything he did made a difference.

———◆———

What Do You Bring to the Table?

Value is not a relative thing based upon how you are viewed in the world. It's innate. Only you determine your value. Your value doesn't increase or decrease based upon someone else's inability to see it. You determine your own value; you decide how to use it. You need to see it, know it, own it, and share it. This is how you access your super power. We all have a super power. Our contribution is finding and sharing our passions and purpose in whatever way is possible.

"When you cease to make a contribution you begin to die."
                                        - Eleanor Roosevelt

Take Aways:

1. When you learn the lesson contained within an unpleasant experience, you will find yourself free of the undesirable emotions associated with the experience.

2. You cannot grow past your own self-definition. If you want to change your behavior, you must first change how you define yourself.

3. Your environment has a great impact on your results. To get better outcomes you must take charge of your environment.

CHAPTER 4: LANGUAGE

> "The more man meditates upon good thoughts, the
> better will be his world and the world at large."
>
> — Confucius

Better Talk Helps Us Walk a Better Walk.

"OK, SO LET'S DIG DEEPER into the areas that drive customer retention," I said as we proceeded to look at what caused lower than expected figures that quarter. "I understand you centralize the customer service for all three of your cleaning service locations, is that right?"

"Yes," my client said confidently. She told me about the calls they received, and she described the "chronic complainers."

I stopped her right there. "What do you call them?" I asked.

"Chronic Complainers" she said matter-of-factly.

"So, how do you think your customer service representatives will serve people who are chronic complainers?" I asked, emphasizing the phrase. "How open will they be to what this person has to say? What tone will they have with the chronic complainers? What patience will they have? How could that patience and open-mindedness impact the first time caller?" I asked, showing the impact of the phrase. I proceeded, "all callers start out at a disadvantage because customer service refers to these people in a derogatory way."

"Wow" she said, "it sounds awful when I hear you say it, but I hadn't been thinking about it that way."

"Look," I said, "I understand that you want to support your staff, and sometimes it can be difficult to work with customers who are upset . . . but they ARE your customers, and the company needs to be happy that they provide feedback because there might be many others who would drop the cleaning service altogether. It's true . . . you may have to invite some clients to leave. But when we label people as essentially being blame-worthy, we have lost our ability to listen and hear the value they may bring."

———◆———

> *When we label people, we fail to make a connection, lose the ability to influence, and miss the lesson.*

Many people use this kind of language all the time and aren't consciously aware of it. Think about it. Do you lovingly refer to your kids as "brats and urchins"? Is your spouse "the old ball and chain"? How about your staff? Are they the "Dream Team" or "The Misfits"?

➤ *The words we choose represent our inner dialogue.*

Our Internal Dialog

Language is the most important aspect of your Championship Psychology. The reason is that **your language defines, reveals, and perpetuates who you are, not only to the rest of the world, but also to yourself!** When you process an event, the very first thing you do, consciously or unconsciously, is to have a conversation with yourself. Without even knowing it, you ask, "What does this mean? How will this affect me? Is this good or bad?" . . . and so on. The questions you ask, the resulting thoughts you choose, and the words you use in this context, will determine how you filter that external event. As a result, your emotions are formed and that expresses itself in your behavior. All of this feeds into how you continue to define yourself. Your words have more power than you realize.

Now, here's the challenging part: We actually have sixteen thousand thoughts a day, one every five and four tenths seconds. It's noisy in there! No wonder it can be so hard to get anything done. Remarkably, studies show that only five percent of those thoughts are new. That means we keep having the same thoughts over and over and over again. Those repetitive thoughts are powerful beyond measure.

Your self-talk will define your results.

"Whether you think you can, or think you can't, you're right."
- Henry Ford

If you begin a task with the mentality that you can't accomplish it, then guess what? You can't. That's the plus and minus of the human mind. You will always make yourself right. If you continue saying to yourself, "I'm not smart/pretty/good enough to do this," then you won't be. Self-talk is what really separates the champions from everyone else. If you want to have a Championship Psychology, it begins with the words you plug into your brain. When you learn to speak the language of productivity, things will begin to fall into place and eventually become automatic. You'll feel better equipped to take on your goals.

The path to learning about language and its impact on our productivity has three steps that you'll need to understand and master:

1) Listen for **Awareness**

2) Get curious with quality **Questions**

3) Understand behaviors to avoid **Self-Sabotage**

AWARENESS

We were given one mouth, two ears, and two eyes, so we should use them in that proportion. Often in conversations, people think ahead to what they will say next and aren't actually listening to what the other person is expressing. How effectively can you communicate with other people if you aren't hearing what they're saying? Besides, noticing language choices in others is generally easier than seeing your own, so this is the perfect place to begin your linguistic awareness.

Listen for Everything

Effective communication can be evaluated by the responses you receive. No matter how much you talk, if you aren't being heard, your message falls upon deaf ears. True listening means not just hearing what is said, but also what is not said. The practice is called "active listening," which means paying attention to the other person as vigorously as possible. If you aren't listening actively, you'll not only miss the words and tone, but you're also going to miss about ninety percent of verbal and non-verbal cues from those around you.

At your next team meeting, look around the meeting room and listen actively. What do you see? Listen for engagement. Who is texting during the meeting? Who is bringing the best energy? Who is listening with interest? Who is leaning back in their seat waiting for the meeting to be over? Use this information to see how you can engage your team even more. You can do this at home, too. Give yourself an assignment and see what you learn from it.

Be Aware

Active listening also includes listening to yourself. In the first part of this chapter, we discussed self-talk to help you listen more carefully to your language.

Sometimes what we say is incongruent with how we are saying it. For example, if during a sales call you said yes, but shook your head no or shrugged, what message did your prospect receive? Did your tone reflect the message you wanted to send? What you say is usually less important than how you say it. In fact, the pitch of your voice can result in your message being the opposite of your words. As a speaker, I was taught that people won't remember what you say, but they will remember how you made them feel.

➤ *Being conscious of your inner dialog will help you find your way back to the center of the productivity zone.*

QUALITY QUESTIONS

Questioning Our Thoughts.

"Are you okay?" I asked my assistant as soon as I saw her. She looked like she had been crying, but was trying to cover it up.

"Yeah, it's just all this stupid drama at school," she said. "I know it LOOKS like I'm in med school, but I swear it's just like middle school part two."

She went on to explain that there had been an incident the night before where another student had accused her of something and called her a disrespectful name. It had gotten under her skin, and I could tell she was internalizing what had been said.

"Why does it upset you?" I asked.

She played nervously with her hair. "I don't want people to think that about me," she said.

"Oh, well I understand that. Megan, I've been meaning to ask . . . are you a dog beater?"

"What?" she asked, looking completely confused.

"Are you a dog beater? Do you beat dogs for fun?"

"Um, no . . ." she said trailing off.

"Well, if I tell someone you are a dog beater, will that make it true? And if I do that, is it you or me who looks bad?"

Asking her those questions allowed her to think about what questions she had been asking herself.

———◆———

Think of questions as filters, gateways we create to process the information we take in. If you ask yourself, "Why am I so stupid," your mind will gladly answer—and not in a flattering way. If you constantly ask yourself accusatory, provocative questions, you will create poor quality filters. Instead, consider reframing your experiences. By asking yourself quality questions, you gain greater and greater insight into the truth of a situation, rather than judging it on initial perceptions.

Often when we look for results, we are searching for the right answers. To get the best answers, we need to ask better quality questions. You will get better results if you focus on asking the right questions rather than looking for the "right" answer. Questions are the most powerful tool we have: So influential, so effective, so accessible . . . and best of all *so simple.*

➤ *Questions direct how you filter events and experiences.*

It is more important to ask the right question than to have the right answer.

If you want to boost your results, ask questions from a place of curiosity rather than of interrogation. You never want to approach people from the position of inquisitor, barking questions at them so they feel like they are being interrogated. Be mindful of the integrity of your questions and how you phrase them.

Questions Have Presuppositions

To understand the five types of questions and what they mean, let's look at them one by one. Consider a conflict situation:

- When you ask a "why" question, that will give you a story, or an excuse, in reference to an event where things didn't go as expected.

- If you ask "how" did this happen, you will get the process.
- If you ask "what" happened, you will get the facts as the person experienced it.
- Asking "who" opens the door to assign blame (not productive in a conflict).
- "When" will help you understand the timing of the situation.

The best leaders not only ask more questions than they give answers, they also rarely ask "who" or "why" questions. They ask "how," "when," and "what" question. The answers you get will only be as good as the questions you ask, so if you want a better answer, ask a better question. Keep in mind that there are situations where it makes sense to ask "why," such as when you are looking for the underlying purpose, and "who," when you are looking for support. By understanding and listening more carefully to the questions you ask, you will be able to ask better quality questions of yourself and others.

SELF-SABOTAGE

Self-sabotage occurs when we engage in thoughts or actions that harm us. Why do we do things that we know are bad for us? Most smokers admit smoking is bad for them, but they still choose to light up. In these cases, the unconscious secondary gain, whether it's getting to take a break for five minutes, socializing with friends, or the satisfaction of the nicotine, is worth more to them in the moment than long-term health concerns. Many times, they have a limiting self-definition that holds them back. There are tons of resources available to smokers who want to quit. Because the factors that contribute to smoking—purchasing cigarettes, lighting one, bringing it to the mouth—are highly visible and therefore easily treated. But what about those bad habits we can't see? Every single day, most people engage in harmful thoughts, actions, and behaviors without even realizing it! The subtlest form of self-sabotage is seen in your self-talk. My dear friend, Dr. Thomas Duncan, refers to them as **ANTs CAN'Ts and BUTs.**

ANTs Are Automatic Negative Thoughts

Someone compliments you about your hair and your inner critic says, "No, not really," or "Are you kidding?" More often than not, it's not as overt as someone sitting at home thinking, "I'm ugly, I'm stupid, and no one likes me." It also goes back to the automatic negative questions we ask ourselves. It could be part of those repetitive sixteen

"What negative self talk is holding you back?"

thousand thoughts a day. That is a form of self-sabotage and although these thoughts and questions currently come automatically, you can reprogram yourself with a software upgrade.

Can'ts and Buts Take Us out of the Game before It Starts

The most common form of self-sabotage comes from the limiting beliefs that drive the many small word choices we make. Consider when a difficult suggestion comes across the table and you immediately think of all the ways this won't work for you. "I understand how it works for them, BUT my business is different, and it won't work for us." Or "I CAN'T manage that right now because . . ." When you come upon a mountain to climb, whether it's in your personal or professional sphere, do you think of it as a challenge (which can be overcome) or an obstacle (which denotes external circumstances that you can't control)? The latter sabotages your success while the former encourages you to keep pushing forward. The words we choose affect or infect and further reinforce limiting beliefs if we allow them to. They influence our identity and how we define ourselves. When Nelson Mandela was asked after being released from twenty-seven years in prison how he survived incarceration, he responded with intensity, "I didn't survive. I prepared." He chose not to allow unfair circumstances define or defeat him, even in his self-talk!

> *Undesired experiences don't define or defeat you;*
  your self-talk does.

Rules and Boundaries

Sometimes, we sabotage our interactions with others and ourselves with the rules we create when we are vulnerable. When we're vulnerable, and feel like trust has been violated in any way, we unconsciously create even more rules (and expectations) to protect ourselves and make people prove their way back in our hearts. But here's the deal. It never works! When we create so many expectations and rules (from limiting beliefs) the relationship cannot thrive; it has no choice but to wither and die, infecting those around it. And that does include our relationship with ourselves.

Consider the following framework for rules and boundaries.

The 'C' at the top of the pyramid represents your communication with yourself and others. There are two parts of effective communication that need balance: 1) rules and 2) boundaries. The line down the middle represents trust. It takes rules and boundaries being in balance to maintain trust. Your boundaries are deal breakers; these are lines no one can cross. They are the baseline expectations of how you want to be treated. Now, think of rules as your specific expectations within your boundaries. They are situational or context specific based upon what you feel is necessary to meet your personal needs. For example, one family may have a boundary that children should not be spanked for discipline. Spanking is not be tolerated. The rules that are created in the family might vary from time outs to positive reinforcement to removal of privileges . . . or any combination of disciplinary measures. And the only way to ensure your babysitter follows your disciplinary practices is to *communicate these rules and boundaries specifically.*

Contracts in business work the same way. They're written to clarify the rules and boundaries. The fact is, in all of our relationships, including the one we have with ourselves, we have unwritten contracts of our rules and boundaries. Things go astray when the unwritten contracts are not clear and/or we are not communicating them.

> *Your boundaries are universal expectations—musts*
>   *and must nots. Your rules are specific expectations*
>   *within those boundaries.*

Most people don't have clarity on their rules and boundaries and, as a result, can't effectively communicate them. Often this lack of clarity increases the level of expectations and the number of rules we live by and creates an unconscious self-abotage of the relationship.

The goal should always be to reach balanced trust. Here is an example of that dynamic:

In the Absence of Trust, The Number of Rules Go Up

My relationship with the CFO was going downhill fast, and I was trying to figure out why, and more importantly, what I could do about it? I was frustrated and sick of trying so hard to get him to work with me. I had just taken over a failing division and digging deep into the causes was critical. But where was he? Off lobbying to be the next CEO, as opposed to rolling up his sleeves with me.

His team was also falling short on their deliverables, doing the bare minimum of corporate accounting. That meant my team and I had to run financial scenarios on our own. I tried to understand why the more we interacted, the more disappointment I felt, and the less our company's objectives were being met. As time went on and his team failed to follow up on the division requests for reporting, it hit me that my expectations of him and his team were increasing rather than decreasing. I started to see that I was putting so many restrictions on the relationship due to my lack of trust that there was no way for our working relationship to be productive. When I finally chose to look at this situation from his perspective, I realized he may have felt threatened by my presence in the company. It was no secret that the CEO was going to be retiring and that he wanted me to replace him. Of course the CFO didn't trust me! Our expectations of one another were mounting and we were creating a situation neither of us could live up to. The rules and expectations became barriers to a productive working relationship.

Sound familiar? Too many unexplained expectations and restrictions create a sense of mistrust in others, particularly in the workplace. When trust is broken, expectations rise, flexibility diminishes, and the relationship withers.

> *Productive and trusting relationships grow through clear expression of rules and boundaries.*

People need to know the boundaries; think of them as the musts and must nots. Trust is earned through common purpose and shared values. But trust can be broken by too many rules and expectations when it becomes too restrictive and shifts the focus away from the intent/values/priorities. When trust is nurtured, relationships thrive and unnecessary rules decrease.

You Still Need to Set Boundaries

That said, maintaining flexibility within relationships is NOT the same as being a doormat or having no rules or expectations. You have values and intentions. And it's normal to have some expectations of the people in your life. These boundaries are the deal breakers. The point is to identify where the limits are and allow more flexibility in all other matters. With the CFO, I had created so many rules that almost anything he did would "break" one of them. I never gave him the benefit of the doubt or multiple ways to show me he was doing his job effectively. It was a lose-lose relationship, because neither of us would be able to get what we wanted or needed. I had to ask myself, what would happen if I let go of those rules?

Perhaps a relationship that was previously "toxic" can grow into something that is healthy or even desirable.

Focus on Intention and Remove Conflict

We had a new head of HR join the executive team. We were going through several changes in the organization, and many people had been asked to leave, or decided to leave, as a result of the changes. Because I was leading the change initiative, many of the people leaving did not have great things to say about me or my involvement. Those first months were challenging with the HR head. The relationship felt strained. Our strained interactions lessened my trust in him.

One day he came into my office and said flat out, "I owe you an apology."

"For what" I asked, totally clueless to what he was thinking.

"I allowed myself to be influenced by the people who were doing exit interviews when I started here. That was unprofessional and wrong. I should have given you the benefit of the doubt and been open to see what I see now from the beginning."

I was blown away. That represented such a high level of integrity from him to say that to me, and from that point on my trust in him went up ten-fold, and my expectations decreased.

———◆———

I never had an issue with him again. We could agree to disagree on a matter but I trusted him one hundred percent.

Stephen M.R. Covey has a book entitled *SPEED OF TRUST*, and I have to agree trust is the element that makes or breaks relationships faster than anything else. I have seen its speed first hand in both directions. The rules and boundaries framework helps you to recognize trust factors faster so you can take action and see how fast creating trust has an impact.

Don't trick yourself into thinking that trust only applies to your personal and business relationships! This also applies to the trust you have in yourself. We sabotage ourselves from a lack of inner trust and create so many rules and barriers that we can't reach the very thing we desire. Take the time to write down all the rules you impose on yourself—for success, for happiness, for feeling productive. Often people find they have pages of them. How would your rules change if you fully trusted yourself and focused on your intention? I go more in depth about this in my online program and live events. Letting go of limitations will give you the freedom you need to find true success.

———◆———

TAKE AWAYS:

1. You are often your own biggest critic. Taking active control of negative self-talk can completely change your life and bring you success!

2. If you want a better answer and better results, ask better questions.

3. More rules and less flexibility can result in toxic relationships and toxic behaviors. The more flexibility you have, the greater your chances are of meeting goals quickly.

CHAPTER 5: PHYSIOLOGY

"You're in pretty good shape, for the shape you're in."
- Dr. Seuss

Treat Yourself Well Now; Avoid Needing Serious Treatment Later

I SAT THERE LOOKING AT my toxicity report. OMG! I only took the test as a means of understanding my client's business better. But the results were astonishing. I thought I had broken the machine, my lead levels were so high. The figures were off the chart! It felt like one of those times when someone tells you they are not sure how you are still walking around with levels like that. Weird, because I considered myself to be pretty fit and healthy. That was a wakeup call to me. I realized that when a symptom appears, chances are it's been brewing underneath the surface for some time. My body, I learned, was on the brink of disaster. I had a choice. I could have left it at that—armed with knowledge but doing nothing about it. But I knew I had to be proactive.

For a year, my doctor prescribed buckets of great big horse pills—the kind that don't even fit into your pill splitter—meant as an oral chelation to lower the lead in my system. I also had to sit through an intravenous drip that took half a day a week for ten weeks. It would have been easy for me to say I didn't have half a day a week to go to chelation (because I didn't). However, I knew that if I refused to take care of this, it could resurface as an even more serious problem later—and imagine how much time I would have to devote to it then. Or maybe worse, I would be out of time! My health scare made me re-prioritize and ask some serious questions. So I ask you: What is brewing underneath the surface for you? Invest in your health now or pay later.

Nothing is easier to take for granted than good health. We often put physiology low on the priority list because when we're feeling fine, we think we don't need to focus on it. Don't be fooled. How your body functions plays an important role in your psychology. You may be asking yourself, "What the heck does my physiology have to do with my psychology?" The answer? Everything. Think about the last time you were sick. How productive were you? Even if you went into the office (and you shouldn't have!), how much did you really get done? When you don't have your health in order, it's very difficult to focus on anything else.

I had a mole that was identified as malignant, and it needed to be removed. Until the surgery was completed and tests confirmed that they got it all, that little discoloration consumed my energy and focus. Night and day, I could barely think of anything else. I got little done at work. Until I had clarity and knew that my health was in order, I was not able to accomplish much else, but that was all right because nothing else mattered at that point. So, rather than fighting against my diagnosis and feeling frustrated and anxious about the health consequences and my apparent lack of achievement, I accepted it and took the time I needed to heal. That in itself felt productive.

Mastering your physiology puts you in a position to bring your best to whatever you do and fully realize your Championship Psychology. It's important to realize that a Championship Psychology doesn't mean being the be-all and end-all every single day. Your best, your one hundred percent will fluctuate based upon your body's health and circumstances day to day. That is okay. You give the one hundred percent you have.

Our Thoughts Affect Our Physiology

John, a friend of mine, was diagnosed with colon cancer. His father had colon cancer, which meant that John needed to be vigilant and get regular checkups. Unfortunately, he didn't (which isn't uncommon), and he was faced with emergency surgery. They took out ten lymph nodes, six of which were malignant. John's good friend, a medical doctor, wanted to be supportive and discuss the details of his condition with him, but John basically told him that he didn't want to discuss it. "Fact is," he said, "I got cancer and that's that. Whatever version doesn't really matter, I've got it. Now I am going to beat it!"

He was prepared to start with chemotherapy, but he refused to talk to anyone about anything that wasn't positive. He just wasn't going to waste his time and energy. He didn't even know he had stage four cancer, nor did he really care. After the surgery, his PET showed no further trace of cancer. None. His doctor said this was unheard of. They all said it was a miracle. But was it?

———◆———

It happens more than we realize. The mind is powerful beyond measure, and there is medical evidence that our thoughts can aid in the healing process when we also take care of our physiology. I'm not saying that you can wish away cancer, but you can envision yourself cancer-free while eating well and taking the appropriate treatments. It can't hurt, and it might help more than you think. Invest in both physiology and psychology today and live a longer happier life.

Although there are many aspects that affect your physical health, to master your physiology I am consolidating them into four parts: Nutrition, Movement, Sleep, and Breathing.

NUTRITION

Eat the Right Fuel

Nutrition refers to anything that you put into your body: food, beverages, vitamins, medication, or any other substances (like nicotine). This is where health really begins. You can have a great exercise regimen, get eight solid hours of sleep a night, and meditate each morning, but if you are filling your body with junk, you won't be healthy. Because this is not a nutrition book,

I won't go into specifics on healthy eating. But let's be clear: What you consume has enormous impact on your well-being. If you want to ride the road to success, you will need the right FUEL. The results we get in our lives depends on what fuel we choose. High performance cars require high performance octane. Similarly, high performance athletes are very focused on their nutrition to get their best performance results.

What's going to give you more energy—a Coke or glass of water? Spoiler alert: It's water! It's so easy to fall into a cycle of filling your body with nothing it needs and everything it doesn't.

Chances are you already know which foods are healthy and which aren't. So what can help you be more consistent in choosing the good stuff? Our biggest challenge today is convenience and fast food. We mentioned environment earlier as a key factor in determining success and failure. You don't have to be in Weight Watchers to develop a healthy diet. Plan your meals and snacks and have them prepared ahead of time. When you reach in the fridge, let it be for vegetables, fruits, and lean proteins that you cut up the day before. Back away from the cake, and don't even think about opening that package of cookies! Stop making excuses and start feeding yourself the foods that do your body good.

➢ *Controlling your environment is one of the easiest way to support productive choices*

MOVEMENT

Movement for Mood

A good friend of mine was going through a difficult time. Over the last few years he put on a lot of weight and had stopped participating in many activities he had previously enjoyed. In other words, he was depressed. He was unhappy in his marriage, and it was eating him up from the inside out.

At the suggestion of his doctor, he began walking each morning. At first just a few blocks, but soon blocks became miles. He began to lose weight, and believe it or not his depression dissipated. Adding that movement into his routine not only gave his body the exercise it needed, it also gave his mind more space to heal, which gave him the motivation to do what he needed to do to be happy!

Movement is a conscious choice to give your body the exercise it needs. This can be as simple as taking the stairs instead of an elevator, or going for a walk on your lunch break.

Movement is essential for your physical and mental health. It makes your body work better in so many ways. It aids your digestion, improves your sleep patterns, and lowers your blood pressure. It even boosts your brain! Everything functions better with some sort of activity. As with my friend, movement can even affect your psyche and self-confidence. People who, due to illness or injury, have to restrict movement to remain in a hospital bed, often experience depression or anxiety in addition to the loss of muscle tone.

The ultimate proof of movement's power is physical therapy, an integral part of nearly all recovery processes. This is because the medical and psychiatric communities recognize the importance of regaining motion for the total healing process.

SLEEP

Sleep and Recharge

The opposite of movement is rest and relaxation. Living in the always-connected, always-on world of the Internet, it's easy to justify sacrificing sleep for production. Believe me, I know how easy it is to just keep working. I fall into this trap all the time. For years, I lived by the "sleep when you are dead" motto often working twenty-four-hour days. There's always "just one more thing" you could do before bed. But after you've done that one thing, guess what? There will be another "one more thing," and another after that.

Make sleep non-negotiable. It's the time when your body has the opportunity to heal and recharge. Trying to go on too little sleep is like trying to drive a car that is out of fuel. Fumes might carry you for a few miles, but in the end you'll wind up stranded on the side of the road.

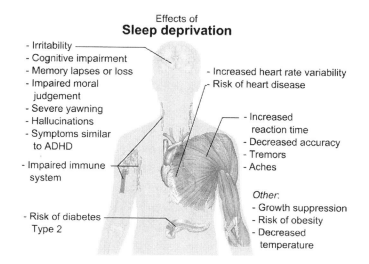

Effects of
Sleep deprivation

- Irritability
- Cognitive impairment
- Memory lapses or loss
- Impaired moral judgement
- Severe yawning
- Hallucinations
- Symptoms similar to ADHD

- Impaired immune system

- Risk of diabetes Type 2

- Increased heart rate variability
- Risk of heart disease

- Increased reaction time
- Decreased accuracy
- Tremors
- Aches

Other:
- Growth suppression
- Risk of obesity
- Decreased temperature

Cultural Imprint

Sleep deprivation is the new normal. In a world where information is constantly at our fingertips, emails are delivered to our phones at all hours, and our attention spans have shrunken so much that we expect immediate responses and results, it's hard to let go and get the rest your body and brain need. But it's essential to make sleep a priority, or your body and mind might flip a switch and cause you to shut down pre-emptively. And how productive will you be then?

If you're like most successful people, you keep a to-do list. Before you decide to give up another minute of sleep, look at each task and ask: "Does this ABSOLUTELY have to be done by tomorrow morning? Is it truly urgent?" Most of the time, the answer will be no.

If you are well-rested, you will get considerably more done than if you are exhausted. So taking eight hours to get some good sleep will actually result in more accomplishment at the end of the day than if you had pulled an all-nighter! Your own experience surely already tells you this is true.

Less Sleep Increases Stress

Lack of sleep lowers our cognitive ability, and we become more susceptible to emotional triggers. For example: you eat more, and make poor food choices, when you are tired. The inability for people to control their emotions and (as a biological result) their heart rate is the main reason for inconsistent performance.

What causes an amazing athlete to suddenly "choke" when he gets out on the field? The simple answer is the inability to manage stress in the heat of the moment. He doesn't align the three types of focus, which we'll discuss in detail in the next chapter. By failing to stay focused and keep his attention on the techniques and process of the task, he lessens the likelihood of success.

When your heartbeat goes up, you probably start to breathe shallowly and inconsistently. For all intents and purposes, you stop breathing at random intervals and your stress level rises higher and higher.

> ➤ *Stress is the number one killer of our performance on AND off the playing field.*

BREATHING

Breathing Controls Your Heartbeat

So how do we control our heartbeat? It's simple. Anyone who's watched a Jane Fonda workout tape will remember her saying, "Don't forget to breathe!" Well, that seems logical, doesn't it? "OBVIOUSLY I'm breathing" you might be thinking. I do that automatically. Well, you'd actually be surprised at how often you're not doing it properly.

When we're stressed, our heart beats faster. It's important to control our heart rate as much as possible because our ability to access our mind goes down as our heart rate goes up. Once our heart rate goes to one hundred twenty beats per minute, the average person is no longer mentally sharp. At one hundred fifty beats per minute, our brain goes into fight or flight mode, focusing strictly on survival. That's where we lose access to our full intelligence.

"When our emotions are high our intellect is low."
- Steven Linder, Founder of Neuro-Strategies

And yet, managing that stress in the moment can be as simple as taking a few deep breaths. We tell children who are angry to take a deep breath because it works!

Try this whenever you're feeling overwhelmed. Breathe in on a count of seven and out on a count of fourteen. Repeat that ten times and your heart rate will lower, your stress will go down, and your clarity will return.

Better breathing can even boost our attention and improve our focus. While you're listening to other people, breathe in more deeply. This will slow you down and improve your listening skills, which will, in turn, create a better connection. In other words, just breathe.

TAKE AWAYS:

1. It's easy to trade healthy for convenient, but you'll pay for it later.

2. Sleep is an essential recharge; don't miss out.

3. Being in control of your physiology supports the control of your emotional state.

4. Take deep breaths more often to control your emotional state and create clarity and focus.

CHAPTER 6: FOCUS

"To conquer frustration, one must remain intensely
focused on the outcome, not the obstacles."
- T.F. Hodge

Gotta Have It

HAVE YOU EVER WANTED SOMETHING so badly that there
was nothing you wouldn't do to get it? With singular
focus, did you do whatever it took to earn your prize? I have.
When I was living in Switzerland, I signed up for a five-day hike
with my friends through the Swiss Alps. It was a mapped trek
and each day we had to walk a fixed number of miles to get to

where we would be sleeping for the night. When we first arrived at the starting point, we found out that the tourism association for the area was sponsoring a contest to win an event-exclusive vest. From the moment I heard about the vest, I knew I had to have it. It would be an emblem of all my hard work and effort, and I would wear it like a badge of honor. But winning the prize was not simple. We had to make the hike in a set number of days and collect stickers associated with each restaurant, ski lift, and hut on the map in the region. It might sound easy, but actually getting to those stops added two hours to the five-and-a half hours of hiking that we were already doing each day. In other words, we added another thirty-six percent of walking and climbing each day. But it didn't matter because we were completely focused on our prize.

I had my first challenge the first day when I put on my hiking boots. The sole had separated from the shoe and was hanging by only a thread. "Really?" I thought. "We haven't even started and I may be already giving up that vest." We were in the middle of nowhere, about to handle some pretty steep climbs, and these boots weren't going to work. I was lucky enough to get a pair of rentals from the hut where we stayed. Apparently, this was not the first time they had seen this happen. The boots fit but not perfectly. They hurt, actually. But I didn't give it another thought. My purpose and mission were clear.

The next day we came to a very narrow path along the edge of a drop off with only a thin wire to act as a barrier between us and a death plunge. One of my friends was afraid to go down this path, so we had to turn back. But the vest! What about the vest?! The way around would add three hours to our hike, and it was impossible to access that hut on this trip. Instead of bypassing that destination, we brainstormed and thought of ways to get the sticker that awaited us in the restaurant on the other side. Lesson learned? When you want something badly enough you get creative.

We saw some others about to enter the trail and we started talking to them. They, too, were collecting the stickers and were headed to the top of the mountain where we were scheduled to be overnight. Why not collaborate! We told them about our challenge of getting across and asked if they could get that sticker for us, and we could get them one from the lower restaurant where we were headed next. They happily agreed and we were really pleased with ourselves for finding a solution.

At the end of the five days, we were so tired and our feet were so sore that we barely made it to the last restaurant. Luckily they had scooters we could ride to the village center, which was a welcomed bonus. It would have been much easier to do that hike without the side trips, but being focused on a goal brought us the energy we needed to finish as well as an added sense of accomplishment. To this day, I wear that vest with pride, signifying one of the most memorable experiences in my life. Without that clear goal, I wonder if it would have been as fun of a trip.

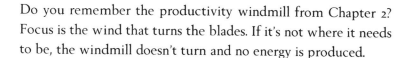

Do you remember the productivity windmill from Chapter 2? Focus is the wind that turns the blades. If it's not where it needs to be, the windmill doesn't turn and no energy is produced.

Three Types of Focus

There is more to focus than meets the eye. Actually there are three primary types of focus:

1. STRATEGIC FOCUS

2. MENTAL FOCUS

3. ATTENTION OF FOCUS

When we manage these in alignment, we're able to attain greater consistency and clarity about what is really important to us and how to achieve it. My hiking trip was an example of aligning the three types of focus. With a clear goal/objective, we made a plan for how we would get all the stickers, and our mental focus enabled us to remain flexible to overcome our challenges and keep our attention on one foot in front of the other.

STRATEGIC FOCUS

Strategic Focus means staying goal-oriented and keeping the big picture at the top of the mind. This implies that your focus is aligned with your purpose, asking the question, "Will this effort directly further my results in reaching my goal? What is the best way to accomplish this?" Even more important, "Will this create leverage to reach the goal faster?" If you can answer "yes," then it is a strategic benefit to you. You always want to work from a strategic perspective. Strategy beats tactics every time!

Because many entrepreneurs struggle with the difference between strategy and tactics, let me make the distinction. A tactic is a specific action. A strategy is the plan and can be executed with individual tactics.

➢ *A tactic may win the battle, but it will never win the war.*

Fixating on one part of a process, without keeping the big picture in mind, is simply using tactics, and it won't be as successful. For example, let's say you want to increase your Internet presence. You can strategize on how to get your name out there across all media, work on consistent messaging to your target audience, and identify where your target market actually is. This will involve several small actions that all contribute to the whole.

The more strategic you become, the better able you are to create sustainable growth in your company and in your life. Most entrepreneurs are deeply involved in the operation of the business, so much so that they spend the day reacting to urgencies of the day-to-day business. Instead of running the business, the business is running them.

Unfortunately, urgencies and emergencies are rarely growth drivers and have you implementing unconnected tactics as you look to grow your business. In sales, I often call this the "spray and pray" approach.

A new client of mine was very excited about the Search Engine Optimization (SEO) work they were doing. Of course, that excitement started to diminish when they found that although the SEO was working and their site was getting more traffic than ever before, they weren't making sales. What's the point of traffic if you can't convert those views to clicks and sales? As it turned out, their website had the wrong messaging, but they were so focused on the SEO that they never put time and resources into improving the web pages. By itself, that SEO was just an un-aligned tactic. However, had it been implemented in conjunction with other marketing (such as improving the website and making sure the message was clear) it would have been a part of an effective strategy. So, what are you looking to achieve with that action or series of actions? You are going to get the best bang for your buck when you can look at the big picture and make sure all your steps are sequentially planned, congruent, and well thought out in relation to your overall goals. Focus on the right thing at the right time. Yes, you may get results from that single action, but are you achieving what you really want and/or need? Are you getting consistent results? That's the difference between people being busy and people being productive. Busy doesn't increase overall long-term achievement. Being productive does.

MENTAL FOCUS

Mental Focus is the ability to control our own filters. Our filters are how we see the world. The reality we create for ourselves. The meaning we give to events in our lives. These filters are created from past experiences, previous decisions, the questions we ask ourselves, and our values and beliefs.

➢ *Filters determine the meaning we give an event.*

In Chapter 3 we talked about how language can influence your entire outcome. Much of achieving a positive mental focus is learning to manage your emotional response in the moment and being able to use the language of productivity in practice. In my hiking story, there were many situations where I could have become psyched out, making an emotional decision to stop or panic. Climbing up a steep rock face in the rain, I had to put away any doubt quickly and focus on climbing. There were a few areas where we had to jump over a crevasse, and my vision was seeing me land on the other side, instead of plummeting to my death. It is amazing how laser-focused you can get when you really need to be. You can block everything out and align your strategic focus and mental focus to provide great strength in the present.

We've all heard stories about people who lift cars off their loved ones. Their thoughts are simply "I must!" versus "I can't." We can do incredible things when we have control over our mental focus.

When you go in for a surgical procedure Dr. Michael Smith, that laser kind of focus is what you hope for from him. While he's removing your spleen, you'd like to think that he's not pining about the split-up with his girlfriend. You want to know he's had a good eight hours of sleep under his belt. If there's a slight complication, you want him not to be thrown off, but focused and present to serve you.

Guess what? You can focus like this in your business and at home. And, like you with your surgeon, your clients and family expect it from you as well.

What is the biggest thing that holds us back from positive mental focus?

Fear

Don't be confused; fear is not the same thing as caution. Think of caution as risk management: understand the risk and evaluate the possible outcomes so that you can minimize an undesirable result. When we fail to make decisions, caution

"Have another look, it was just a paper tiger"

becomes fear. When you freeze, lose sight of the path ahead, or feel unable to take action, then you are letting fear dictate your results. You are no longer in control. As a leader, when you act (or don't act) out of fear, you lose the respect of your team and your ability to lead effectively diminishes rapidly. Fear also shows itself in procrastination and perfectionism.

Of course, recognizing the fear for what it is won't eliminate it, just as recognizing sadness, anxiety, or anger won't make those emotions vanish either. Obviously, you experience those feelings at one time or another, especially when you're under stress. After all, you're human.

> *The trick is to remember that your reaction is completely within your control.*

At my Productivity Accelerator Bootcamp, I teach in depth the process of managing emotional triggers in your environment that lead to emotional reactions in depth. Here are two of the most important take-aways from that training to start you on the path to productivity:

- In stressful situations, take a "time out" and consider the situation from a neutral third-party perspective. Disassociating yourself from the event will remove the emotion. Seeing it from the point of view of someone uninvolved will help you find clarity and truth.

- Ask better quality questions. This will help you to understand what is triggering the emotion, and see beyond the emotion to solutions.

With practice, both of these techniques can be done in a split second to direct your response and get the results you desire.

ATTENTION OF FOCUS

Attention of focus is about being fully present. This means concentrating on and in the moment. Your attention of focus is affected or infected by your purpose, language, and physiology. All of these elements are closely intertwined to create your mood, which directly influences the level of your energy and the quality of attention you give to any particular task or moment. My dear friend Dr. Tom and I call this ability to be present the RFN (Right Frickin' Now).

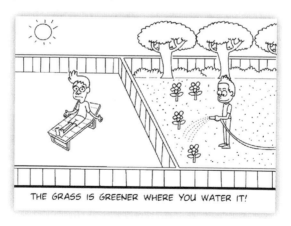

THE GRASS IS GREENER WHERE YOU WATER IT!

One morning I had a massive screaming match with my three-year-old son. When I got in the car on my way to work, I was upset by the emotional interaction. I got even more upset when I realized that he was only three and that he wasn't behaving typically. What created this argument?

It was **me**! **My** stress. **My** lack of presence. All he wanted was my attention, and I wasn't giving him what he needed. Shame on me!

Being present in the moment means not being distracted by environmental or emotional influences that you know aren't important. What are the process steps and standards to be adhered to in the moment? For a football player, his focus should be on the upcoming play, where he's supposed to be on the field, the pattern, the block or pass he's supposed to execute. It requires watching how the play unfolds and moving and reacting as necessary IN THE MOMENT.

If his mental focus is still on a past play, he will be distracted or confused. If he isn't clear on the strategic objectives of the play, he will also be sidetracked. If he concentrates too much on the mental focus or the strategic focus, he denies himself the ability to respond in the moment.

Multitasking Is Not Efficient

What about your attention at work? One of the biggest culprits preventing you from paying your full attention is multitasking. We know it distracts and disperses our focus, but it continues to be a growing drain of our productivity. Let's face it. You can't do everything well at the same time.

> ➤ *Twenty-eight percent of our time is lost in redirecting and refocusing our attention!*

As a result, the quality of our work suffers; we make more mistakes, and make poor decisions. All of this adds even more time and increases our overall costs. No efficiency here! Too often, people applaud multitasking as a highly desirable trait. But the real productivity achieved through focused monotasking, doing one thing at a time.

——◆——

Technology Is a Blessing and a Curse

There are countless ways that we waste time daily by allowing our attention to go where it shouldn't. Modern technology creates amazing opportunities for productivity but just as many opportunities to waste time and divert attention (Facebook and YouTube come to mind.) Keep your focus aligned on the task at hand, stay present, and you'll be able to do twice as much in half the time!

Finding It Hard to Stay Motivated and Focused?

Here are two tips to stay motivated and focused:

1. Use a timer to clearly limit the amount of time you will work on something and set a clear goal or result for that time frame. This will help you to create some pressure and attention to block out distractions, knowing after the bell you will have time to do other things.

2. Go work somewhere else where there are no distractions—a meeting room, the library, the kitchen table, or a Starbucks. Changing your environment will help you to break patterns of distraction.

Take a moment to consider what you could do with all that new-found time. Think about why this is important and what part of the whole this part represents. With the extra time you could walk to the park with your children. Go out to dinner with your spouse. Take some well deserved "me time" to read a book, go to the gym, or do whatever makes you feel calm and happy. You could do all that and more, but only if you take charge of the RFN!

TAKE AWAYS:

1. Strategy will always be more powerful than tactics. If your plan isn't working, analyze it to see if it is tactically or strategically based.

2. You determine the meaning of the events in your life.

3. Aligning strategic focus, mental focus, and attention of focus will create laser focus for the best results.

CHAPTER 7: WINNING STRATEGIES

"The worst enemy of the strategist is the clock. Time trouble ... reduces us all to pure reflex and reaction, tactical play. Emotion and instinct cloud our strategic vision when there is no time for proper evaluation."

- Garry Kasparov

"I JUST CAN'T PUT MY finger on why we're not closing more business," John, the CEO of an event management company said to me. "It's not like we aren't getting invited to submit proposals. We have a great reputation, which gets us in the door. And right now we must have fifty RFPs or bids, in various stages of development."

"Well, that sounds good, but you're not converting them into sales. Your conversion rate is lower than twenty percent." I clarified. Truly, the company's problem was even worse than that.

In the last year, most of the sales this company had closed were yielding smaller margins. In order to make their volume goals, the sales people were cutting prices and offering discounts. Discounting is tactical, not strategic. Sure, they were packaging them as "promotions," or wrapping them into "incentives bonuses." But the result was the same, a lower percentage of profit per sale year over year, no matter how they described it. In this highly reactive mode, what they didn't see was they were actually destroying their value proposition in the eyes of their prospects.

In addition to poring over the company's sales numbers, I also reviewed their value proposition, their website, and all of their marketing materials. At my next meeting with John, there was no way to sugarcoat my analysis.

"I have to be direct. There's nothing in your marketing or your processes that differentiates your company from your competition," I said.

John looked at me as if I'd grown a third eye. "Penny, it is our customer service and the value of our in-depth knowledge to manage events and bring them in on time and within budget. That's what makes us different," he countered, a bit defensive.

"Yes, I understand," I said. "But everyone says their value proposition is the customer service and their expertise. If you don't develop something different in how you deliver service or educate people on the difference—like a proprietary method to make you stand out—you'll continue to be treated as a commodity. That's why price has become your only form of competition. Getting new business will remain a struggle with long sales cycles and diminishing margins."

Often companies have a message, but that message doesn't make them stand out. There's no real differentiation and no leverage to create consistent, sustainable growth. Put another way, they have no real strategy. Most people are not fully aware of the difference between strategy and tactics. And then that shows up in everything they do.

A year later, John's business is now booming, and their pipeline full of quality leads that they are closing sixty percent faster and at a conversion rate of over thirty percent. What led to the turnaround was their new Event Efficiency Assessment. That differentiation allows them to show off their knowledge and gets their foot in the door for more interesting prospects. It functions like a home energy audit, where the company assesses the events risk, overall cost efficiency, and the quality of the experience for their prospects. This specialized approach has led them to landing bigger projects with better partners. It helped them educate their prospects on the most important aspects of event management and their unique skill set. This educational process created a clear differentiation, which closed more sales and allowed them to charge full price for their expertise, raising their margins.

---◆---

Forest or Trees?

We've all heard the expression, "He couldn't see the forest for the trees." I'd like you to think about what the author, German poet Marcel Odenbach, really meant. He was referring to the kind of person who's so fixated on the individual trees, he can no longer see the forest, and is likely to get lost. He's not in touch with his goals, and he isn't going to move forward. This is a common occurrence for people who are stressed and overwhelmed. This kind of person is just focusing on what is in front of them and hoping to survive the day.

See the Forest and the Trees

Alternately, someone who sees the forest only as a whole may neglect individual trees. True, having the big picture is important, but we also need to be able to put that into context and be able to break it down into implementable chunks.

The forest may represent your company goals, or even just the goals for a large project. The trees within it are the individual tasks that will get you to that goal. If you neglect the individual trees because they seem insignificant to the whole, you'll quickly find that your forest won't thrive. On the other hand, if you devote all of your time and resources to singularly focusing on one tree, you won't reach your destination in a timely manner—if you even get there at all.

> ➤ *The Core Elements of a Winning Strategy Are:*
>   *Planning, Process, and Priority.*

A lack of clarity in these three areas will push you right out of the productivity zone because it creates stress and a feeling of being overwhelmed. When you're unable to determine your course of action, and when or how you will do it, you are focused on only the forest: Frozen like a deer in the headlights.

Planning Creates Focus

Let me be clear. *Without strong and effective planning you won't achieve your goals, at least not without consequence.* In this chapter we're going to focus on how to plan productively.

Think about our earlier windmill example. Without an effective strategy, the blades will certainly turn, but they will turn **veeeeery slooooooooowly**. Oh, you'll still probably get some results; but with a great plan, you could double or even triple them . . . in half the time. So why settle?! In terms of the Productivity Curve, when you don't have an outline in your head, you might find yourself in the optimal zone occasionally, but you'll frequently slip back out of the zone because nothing is anchoring you there.

Process Creates Leverage

Think of process as how you do what you do. When it's standardized, it becomes the mechanism that takes plans and turns them into results. It oils the gears, and the windmill turns smoothly. But if it's weak or inconsistent, it's like tossing a wrench into the gears! All the plans in the world won't get you much closer to your goals without a clearly defined process for implementing them and creating sustainability. Imagine scheduling a road trip, but not putting a process in place to fuel up the car. The best map ever designed won't make your car move forward; it can only tell the car where to go once it's moving. Planning sets the standard, and process implements the standard through structure, so that the standard can be met consistently.

Priority Powers Momentum

Understanding your priorities gives you direction and flexibility. But to truly comprehend what a priority is, you must first understand the difference between URGENT and IMPORTANT. Learning to understand and separate the two, and act accordingly, can completely change your results.

A lack of clear priorities is what keeps people out of the productivity zone. On the side of perfectionism they are so caught up in the emergencies they neglect important tasks and values. Crowd pleasers—like John earlier in this chapter—take on too much and try to do it all themselves. They create a false sense of urgency around every job, unable to distinguish what's urgent from what's important. On the procrastination side of the productivity curve are people who find the urgent tasks too overwhelming, so the **TOP** of their to-do list never gets done, even though the work further down the list does. By focusing on less mandatory business—handling second-tier responsibilities—they're able to delay what should come first. In both cases, these people are very, very busy, but rarely productive. When your priorities are out of whack or you lack clarity, how can you meet your goals without sacrificing something or someone?

> ➤ *Remember that all elements of a Winning Strategy are built on top of Championship Psychology.*

The sequence matters: Imagine you want to bake a cake. You add all the ingredients in a bowl and immediately throw it in the oven before mixing it up. You aren't going to get the result you were expecting. By getting your Energy Management and Championship Psychology under control, you will be able to maximize your Winning Strategies.

TAKE AWAYS:

1. Winning Strategies is made up of Planning, Process, and Priority.

2. Planning creates focus.

3. Process creates leverage for growth.

4. Priorities will power your momentum.

CHAPTER 8: PLANNING

"In preparing for battle I have always found that plans
are useless, but planning is indispensable."
                                    - Dwight D. Eisenhower

Enthusiasm Is No Substitute for Planning and Preparation: A Case History

M Y CLIENT SUSAN WAS EXCITED about the new cosmetic
company she was working with. I could feel her passion
as she explained what the products had done for her skin and
the amazing results she had with people who suffered from
rosacea, eczema, and other skin problems. "After weeks of
discussions and negotiation, the CEO is willing to give me

distribution rights on the East Coast. I can make this really big," she said.

I was excited for her, but I've learned enough in my own business to not be too emotionally involved in the product or the situation. I wanted her to slow down and think this through.

"Before you invest any further time and effort," I advised, "I'd like you to discuss a few things with the CEO about the manufacturer. Ask targeted questions and listen—really listen—to what is said. Don't just hear what you want to hear. Think of it as surveillance for your company."

In Susan's case, I proposed she find out their current capacity and how many units they are producing. "What is the maximum number of orders they can fill without having to make further investments in their infrastructure? What plans for expansion to their infrastructure do they see, and in what time frame? If they really do have a great product on their hands, they may need to ramp up quickly and you want to be sure they can deliver on your orders on time." I was asking the kinds of challenging questions I wanted my client to ask her prospective partner. "Susan, you've had some initial discussions with Costco and the orders could get large. Have you discussed the numbers they'll need per month?"

Bursting the Bubble to Make Room for Reality

"I hadn't really thought of that. Is it important at this stage?" Susan asked, as if I had burst her excitement bubble.

"Yes, now is the time. Before you invest a lot of hours and money, you have to think several steps ahead. You need to run scenarios with them to project how the business will grow and what lead times are needed to increase capacity. As a team, you need to plan out the future before it happens. Think through what can go wrong and what can go right, and know how you will handle successes and setbacks."

I was trying to help Susan see that if she didn't have strategies in place before challenges arise, it can create a great deal of stress and overwhelm for her and the rest of the team. People stop thinking logically. Finger pointing soon replaces constructive problem solving. Conversely, when you're prepared for Plans A, B and C, you're more equipped to be flexible. You need flexibility to effectively and efficiently run your business.

I've seen this before. People get so excited about the potential, they forget to ask many of the essential questions to safeguard that the infrastructure can support the demand. Delivery guarantees should be in your contract. Always.

"Susan, can you see why this would be important?" I asked.

"Yes, but I trust them," she said, naively. "Is this really necessary?"

Her question was optimistic. My goal was to make her realistic.

"Of course you trust them, or you wouldn't be doing business with them," I said. "But things change, priorities shift, and business situations evolve. You need to protect your most important assets right now—your time and money. You need to write down your expectations and ensure everyone is accountable for their part. This will secure both of your investments in the project going forward. No one wants to plan for failure; you are simply mitigating your risk by looking at the what-ifs. I can tell you from my own experience that a lack of clarity in the terms of a contractual relationship is not in your best interest. Especially if things don't go as planned. Contracts with clear terms are what keep everyone honest. That's why we have locks on doors, right?"

The Outcome: Give More Time to Critical Thinking

Susan's initial skepticism yielded to my experience. Or so I thought. She went back and forth with the CEO to clarify these elements. I didn't find out until later that none of the items I discussed with her were actually spelled out in her contract. She had discussed them with the CEO, but there was no written plan or systemic follow-ups in place.

Full speed ahead, she began creating commercials, participating at trade shows, and building a sales team to get this East Coast business off the ground. She was starting to get substantial prospects interested—spas, cruise lines, and Costco. Lucky for Susan, these deals would take some time to materialize.

In the meantime, the agent in Canada was making significant headway with product sales and manufacturing. And the cosmetic manufacturer couldn't carry out the smaller sales Susan had booked with local spas and individuals. Her small orders were not getting filled in a timely manner. Sometimes they weren't getting filled at all! Susan found out firsthand how important it is to ask the right questions from the start and understand not only HOW you are going to make the sales, but also how you will DELIVER on them. Poor planning can make or break a business and can prove to be very costly.

———◆———

When we re-visit Championship Psychology, it is clear that strategic planning encompasses purpose (the "what" and "why" we are doing what we are doing), and the need for specific clearly expressed goals. "Seeing the forest for the trees" is a great analogy because it illustrated for us the balance required between strategy and tactics (reviewed in the Focus section of

Championship Psychology). We have to understand the types of trees and know that we have all the equipment—plus the skills and resources—to handle the quantity we aim to produce. These elements are part of Strategic and Operational planning.

Eat the Elephant One Bite at a Time

The first step is to clearly define your intended outcomes. Once those are identified you can break them down into small pieces, so you can focus on taking down one tree at a time. Your approach must be founded in your vision and purpose, seeing the big picture as it comes together, task by task. I'm not going to go into specific business and sales strategies in this chapter (although I do conduct workshops on these topics). But I want to explore what makes a good strategy and put you on the path to developing your own. Both strategic and operational planning require you to ask quality questions.

The Best Questions Help You to Better Understand What You're Doing at Micro and Macro Levels:

- "What do we need to deliver in an efficient and effective manner?"
- "Where is the market headed, and what are the needs of my prospects and customers today?"
- "How have your goals/priorities changed, and will they change again?"

➤ *A strong plan is both strategic and operational.*

Every minute you spend identifying and readying your objectives can save you hours later on.

We've all been in situations where we didn't chart our course before getting started. When that happens, we wind up spending an exorbitant amount of time and energy going the long way around. The question is: What did we learn? And why don't we apply what we know?

For the purposes of this book, let's break planning down into three main sections: Strategic Planning, Operational Planning, and Organizational Planning.

STRATEGIC PLANNING

Strategic plans start with clearly knowing what you want to achieve.

Clarify your vision

Clarity of vision and purpose creates real ownership and positive accountability, which are central elements of a Championship Psychology. James Collins is credited for coming up with the concept of The Big Hairy Audacious Goal (BHAG) in his book *BUILT TO LAST: SUCCESSFUL HABITS OF VISIONARY COMPANIES.* BHAGs are meant to shift how we do business, the way we are perceived in the industry, and possibly even change the industry itself. Once you have your BHAG you must identify an approach for how to make it happen.

Know Your Environment and Your Market

Strategic plans look at the forest and understand the environment. What trees tend to grow well in this climate and soil? Is the whole forest the same? What types of trees are here now and what else is possible and desirable? What wild-life is present? Are there any hunting restrictions? In other words, you need to evaluate your business, products and services, potential markets, competition, differentiation, and the characteristics that will make your endeavors successful.

Set Your Goals

Now that you know your long term vision and BHAG and the environment you are in, it is time to get clear on those short term, mid-term, and long term goals. Business plans are not just for big companies. Business planning will bring clarity for you so that you can bring clarity for your team. And don't think for one second that "team" only means people you employ! Your team can be made up of family, friends, and affiliates too . . . they all need clarity if they are going to help you succeed.

Plan for Growth

What capacity are you currently running at? What needs to be in place for growth and expansion? What resources, skills, and infrastructure need to be present short-, mid-, and long-term to meet your obligations? How will things look in leaner times and in richer times? Knowing this will help you effectively plan your cash flow, budget, and staffing needs.

Sadly, the majority of companies who have strategic plans fail to implement them properly. According to a Fortune magazine cover story, nine out of ten organizations fall short in this important area for many reasons:

- **Sixty percent** of organizations don't link strategy to budgeting.
- **Seventy-five percent** of organizations don't link employee incentives to strategy.
- **Eighty-six percent** of business owners and managers spend less than one hour per month discussing strategy (lack of focus)
- **Ninety-five percent** of a typical workforce doesn't understand their organization's strategy.

Focus on the Forest, but Work Your Way Through It

People have always told me I think differently. If that's true, the reason is that I am strategically focused. I frequently ask myself, "How does this fit in with my strategy? How does this add value to my prospects and customers? How does this support my differentiation? What leverage am I creating?"

Here's an example from my own business of approaching an opportunity by asking the right questions:

I once was asked to join a group of top-notch coaches who were going to offer free twenty-minute sessions on their website. At the risk of offending them, I responded that I definitely wasn't interested, and then I explained why.

A) My Differentiation
I am an elite productivity coach. If I provide a free session on the Internet, I am contradicting my brand positioning.

B) My Target Audience
What types of people will be attracted to the website on average? The attracted prospects probably cannot afford to invest in hiring us. I want to spend my time to target clients who fit my profile.

C) Create Leverage
To reach a wider audience I do a radio show, offer group coaching, and offer online tools. This allows my company to grow beyond the number of hours I can coach. I've created targeted programs that are affordable at all levels: from a simple assessment, to ongoing accountability in-group sessions twice a month, to live events and elite coaching. The next stage of this system is a certification program for other coaches to provide a lower entry point for one-on-one coaching.

In this case, my strategic plan helped me to turn down an opportunity.

> *Knowing which projects to pass on is as important as knowing which ones to focus on!*

The strategic plan you have created provides you and your team with the approach you need to pursue a specific direction, establish performance goals, and deliver value to all parties involved. However, this is just a map; it doesn't guarantee the preferred results any more than having a map guarantees that the traveler will arrive at the desired destination.

OPERATIONAL PLANNING

Addressing the Individual Trees

What is the end goal? How will you know you have gotten there? How will you know you are twenty-five percent, fifty percent, and seventy-five percent of the way? What specific measurement tools are you using? Who is responsible for each project/task, and how will they document its completion? Strategically, you set up the what and the how. Operationally, you get into the specifics, the individual trees, for clarity of execution.

Set Your Milestones

In previous sections we talked about creating goals. This is where we make them SMART (Specific, Measureable, Attainable, Realistic and Measurable) goals.

It is so easy to set overarching goals and then become overwhelmed. The intent is good, but when a systems leader is frozen or overwhelmed, everything comes to a screeching halt as you or your team fails to act on those goals. I see it all the time. The magnitude of the greater goals is too large to comprehend, and rather than moving forward you hold still, afraid to make the first move.

Planning Small Steps Breaks Down Fear and Overwhelm: A Case Study

Bill had a strong desire to make a huge impact on the world. His dreams were big. He wanted to create a billion dollar foundation for Veterans, but his excuses for not getting started were even bigger. We examined his belief systems to remove the psychological obstacles that kept him from acting on his good intentions. After the barriers were gone, he was so fired up he couldn't wait to take action! He began to describe his vision as he looked toward the future. It was vivid and the details seemed to come clearly to him. He had stepped into it, even if just for the moment. It was invigorating to hear the energy he was ready to put behind this mission. This was his BHAG.

Over the next few weeks I asked him to research how to make this happen and to interview others who had already done it. To my surprise, he shied away from these tasks after being so excited. The thing was, his BHAG was so big that even though he could distinctly see it, it was overwhelming. He felt distracted by the enormity of what he was to achieve. He was frozen with fear, and he lacked clarity on his path.

Do you know anyone who has a vision but can't get his or her head around how to break it down? It happens all the time. Let's take a look at how you breakdown the whole into its components and take those first vital steps forward.

◆

Asking the Right Questions Is the Cornerstone of Effective Planning

Let's recap the questions that drive this whole process. The first and most important question involved in your strategic planning is WHY. This is where you can plan the details of the operation. Second is WHAT, which should include the approach you intend to use to get to those goals. Third question in the sequence is HOW. When people know WHAT, but don't know HOW, they are stopped in their tracks. This is an area that often causes procrastination. Some people have trouble answering a how question. The final question is WHAT IF and/or WHAT NEXT. This is learning by doing. It enables us to foresee challenges and avoid them altogether, or adapt as we go. These last two questions are action driven.

Without answers to these questions you and/or your team may become stalled in procrastination mode. Answer them to be efficient and effective in achieving your targets.

Plan Your Personal Capacity

Some people think that the next step is scheduling. The theory goes, master your scheduling, and you will master your time management. Unfortunately it isn't that simple. Let's focus first on what you do before you build your schedule. Because before you can plan your day/week/month/year, you need to know the depth of your resources and then align them at a high level with your strategy and goals.

➤ *Leveraging capacity for greater productivity means starting with the end in mind and working backwards.*

This is important, not just for large project teams, but individual planning as well.

If It's Not in Your Schedule, It's Not Going to Happen

"Ann" I asked, after we looked over some of the business metrics, "How much time are you blocking out to spend on customer loyalty? Let me look at your calendar to see how you book and allocate your time."

"What?" she said, "I set appointments and have my monthly deadlines listed in my calendar. That is about it."

This is common of entrepreneurs. They don't plan their day, so their day gets away from them. "Do you think keeping your customers is important? What is the cost to acquire a new customer?" I asked her. "You focus all your efforts on acquiring new customers, but you wouldn't have to acquire so many new customers if you kept all the existing ones."

Her eyes lit up as if I had flipped a switch. She had really never considered that keeping clients longer meant not having to work so hard for new ones. However, she was worried that she wouldn't be able to find the time to focus on customer loyalty. I asked her to pull that calendar back out and actually block time for each of her priorities.

I walked her through the capacity planning process, and soon she had scheduled time for all of her priorities. What's more, she realized that she was spending time on tasks that weren't moving her forward, and by removing them from her agenda, she freed up time that she could spend exploring new revenue streams.

Capacity planning can change the way you live your life! If you need help getting started, you can access the business growth spreadsheet in my online training program.

Don't Plan to Use one hundred percent of Your Resources. After All, You'll Need to Sleep!

On the same note, if you're ramping up your business, you need to be aware of the excess resources you might have to ensure you can produce, deliver, or manage whatever it is you are offering. You can really harm your reputation by not having this information in place. I encourage my clients to write out their capacity planning—spell it all out—rather than talk or think about it. Every time we write something out, it generates another level of clarity. I offer them this example as an illustration of how writing it out may make you more aware of how much attention a project needs to be completed.

How Does It Look?

In this case, a hypothetical client wanted to devote ten percent of his resources to marketing. That sounded great, until he wrote down what "marketing" meant to him. Do you think it can be accomplished with ten percent capacity, or will he need to devote more of his time to it?

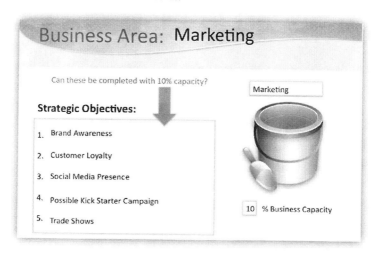

Business Area: Marketing

Can these be completed with 10% capacity?

Marketing

Strategic Objectives:

1. Brand Awareness

2. Customer Loyalty

3. Social Media Presence

4. Possible Kick Starter Campaign

5. Trade Shows

10 % Business Capacity

To begin your planning, start with eighty or ninety percent capacity and work backwards. As you allocate resources to each of your lines of business, subtract that percentage from the whole. You may find that you don't need as much as you thought for each line. You may find that you need to table some projects until you have the ability to attack them successfully . . . or until you can delegate them to someone.

Something has to give or you will remain stuck on either side of the productivity zone—either frozen from overwhelm or burning the midnight oil trying to finish "just one more thing."

Where Is Your Time Going?

I worked with a client who was the CEO of a software company. He came to me because he felt like his work was endless, but nothing was ever getting done. I had him track his time for a few days and we realized that he was spending fifty percent of his day answering email. Fifty percent! After further questioning, we realized that none of these emails were directly impacting his business, worse yet, his assistant could have answered at least half of them, despite his insistence that no one else in the company had the knowledge to respond properly. No wonder his to-do list grew while his business shrank. He wasn't clear on what his time was worth and how much should be dedicated to answering emails. He needed to set up systems to handle frequently asked questions without manual intervention and to delegate the emails that required a response to a member of his staff. Most importantly, he had to stop receiving these messages in his inbox because he felt compelled to answer them.

Once he wasn't bombarded with energy-consuming and distracting letters, he was free to focus on revenue-generating activities and lead the company. The result? Business began growing by leaps and bounds. Knowing how you spend your time and what your time is worth can be the most valuable exercise you can do for yourself. Most people are unaware. No change can occur with out initial awareness.

➤ *Control your environment to support your goals and objectives.*

Things Change, and So Should You

Flexibility. We all know that plans may change—that unforeseen situations may force you to deviate from the program. That is okay because plans are not supposed to be so rigid that you can't adapt. Plans exist to analyze and anticipate what is needed when things are calm and clear. When you get into the thick of a situation, emotions may cloud that situation. The plans you create help to provide guidance and a necessary separation from the excitement of the moment. In business it helps to stay on top of what the competition is doing, where the market is headed, how you will differentiate yourself, and stay the course when distractions arise. In your personal life, these plans act as reference points for financial savings, for discipline in raising your children, and in balancing your day-to-day desires and responsibilities.

You might be thinking it sounds so simple, why don't people see it? Why don't people plan and organize in a way that supports them better? Well, we all have our blind spots. We become emotionally tied to our own stories and excuses. It helps to work with others who can illuminate these autopilot behaviors and call us on our stories, pointing out the ones that aren't supporting us.

———◆———

ORGANIZATIONAL PLANNING

What Are the Roles and Responsibilities That Support Success?

Tim is truly a brilliant man. He has multiple businesses and is very successful at what he does. However, he has consistently made the same mistake over and over. He hired one person to manage his whole back office, from finance to marketing. Although he was selective and put people through a rigorous hiring process, he unconsciously was looking to clone himself not recognizing his own strengths and weaknesses. He found intelligent people, and regardless of the experience or potential they possessed, they were not hired for the skills required for one role. They were hired for several roles. Each of these roles actually fit different personality types. Keep in mind that the primary skill set and disposition of a marketer is about as far away as one can get from a financial person.

Due to his personality type as a visionary and creator, his communication was sparse, his expectations high, and his sense of urgency immediate. This was a recipe for disaster for the incoming team members. For years, he ended up with disappointments and costly mistakes. Finally, he decided to try a new approach to get the right people into his organization. He started to profile them to fit the individual roles he wanted to fill. By hiring for the role and removing some of the emotion from his decision making, he hired the right profile, and his new team is functioning much better.

———◆———

You're Great! (But One of You Is Enough)

The last, but one of the most crucial, aspects of planning is working in collaboration with your **Championship Team**. Like John, it's not surprising to hear that we're often most comfortable around people who are like us. That may explain why we think people who share our point of view, or have had similar work experiences, would fit quite nicely into our company. It's not unusual to see teams of people who mirror the boss's self-image. It's wonderful to feel good about yourself, but a team made up of you-clones is not always the best option. In fact, scratch that: It's never the best solution! Your team *already has you.* What's needed are people who complement each other with the different skills and perspectives, doing the work that *they're* passionate about. Although we all build up adaptive skills to be good at many things, that doesn't mean those are the things we're best suited for. In other words, all new hires should be profiled to ensure the right team fit for their natural disposition.

> ➤ *The best way to build your team is to focus on the roles required for the project, business, or support that you need.*

On a piece of paper or a computer screen lay out the roles and responsibilities of your business, even if you are doing them all yourself. If money, time and resources were no object what roles would you have supporting you? What mentors and advisors would you have? Imagine your successful business in three years and the great team you have built that enabled you to get there. Describe the values, the culture, and the roles of your business.

I use a profiling program called Talent Dynamics to ensure the team is properly balanced and that each player is in the right position.

A Happy Team Is a Healthy Team

Once you have a great team, keeping them is just as important. Unless you manage, engage, and recognize your team effectively, good people can be hard to hold on to. Many employers cultivate an environment of fear or internal competition, which actually creates a destructive culture. Communication gaps, aggression or apathy, as well as self-sabotage is usually the result. Some managers are fooled because initially competition may appear to work, but it isn't sustainable. The real question you need to ask is, "What is the best way to inspire and involve my staff to get optimal collaborative results?"

> *Your employees don't need to compete, they need to engage.*

Building the right team, communicating clearly, trusting openly, and interacting productively are essential. Earlier, we discussed the value of engagement and the necessity of inspiring your team.

When the right people are in the right roles, a great leader's job is to remove the obstacles that keep people from their own motivation. Therefore, when delegating any role or responsibility, you need to make sure your people have not only the responsibility but also the authority to carry out that role. Micromanagement will squash the spirit of the best people and eventually yield negative results.

> *Creating engagement is the LEADER'S responsibility!*

Involving the team or team leaders in as much of the development of business strategies and processes as possible will go a long way to creating personal ownership and enthusiasm.

TAKE AWAYS:

1. Overwhelm and overloaded are not the same thing.

2. Planning reduces stress and eliminates overwhelm and overload.

3. The best teams complement each other, so plan for well-rounded teams.

4. Collaboration beats competition for engagement and sustainable results.

CHAPTER 9: PROCESS

"Our standards are so high here, I have heard people say we have double standards"

> "I think a major act of leadership right now, call it a radical act, is to create the places and processes so people can actually learn together, using our experiences."
> - Margaret J. Wheatly

Without a Process Your Plans Are Just Good Ideas

I HAVE A CHIROPRACTIC CLIENT who has seven locations. The business has built a support structure with team leaders and a doctor who oversees training in all their offices, as well as an office manager at the home office. The idea behind that level of oversight is to provide the staff and doctors easy access to administration so that they can quickly and efficiently handle any concern. The issues can range from questions about patients, to problems with billing, and of course, interoffice conflicts. Sounds wonderful, right? But their comprehensive framework lacked a process and did not clarify responsibilities or authority. The intent was there, but they had no protocols to back it up. This happens when people assume that everyone understands the intention of the new roles and fail to document and communicate the roles and responsibilities.

Who Is Responsible?

During a meeting, the owners told me about a recent situation where one staff member had a problem with how a doctor was printing a document. At its core, the issue was minor. The staffer went to the team leader who offered to look into the problem. But the staffer wasn't satisfied so she went to the office manager and three other doctors. By the end of the day, five separate people had spent valuable time talking with the "offending" doctor about a simple printing problem. Can you imagine how frustrating it was for him to get reprimanded five times in one day over a printing issue?

Naturally, I spoke to the owners about optimizing an escalation process so it could be communicated to everyone involved. If a member of the staff took a problem to someone other than the responsible person, the issue would be properly redirected to the correct responsible person. When everybody is clearly advised, everybody can support the defined process.

Avoid Procrastination and Perfectionism

Processes improve the quality of products or services by standardizing the steps that lead to a specific outcome. That's true, by the way, for any area of your life. The goal of a process is to ensure a repeatable result. Ideally, it results in shorter delivery times and better value.

In the first chapter we talked about the Productivity Curve. Once we define processes and systems, they support us. That clarity propels us to action, allowing us to avoid the procrastination side of the curve. It also reduces the stress and pressure of doing "just one more thing." It sounds funny but process will set you free. Once you begin executing within a championship process, you will have quality, responsibility, rules, and boundaries built in.

Process = Efficiency

Having a process systemizes the work to be performed; it defines the inputs and outputs, roles and responsibilities. Standardization improves the consistency of the delivery to ensure that all clients receive identical quality. McDonald's is a great example. Regardless of whether or not you like their product, it's easy to see that their business model is effective. Every burger and at every store is the same. No matter where you are in the world, you can expect the same meal and dining experience at any McDonald's. This consistency, created through process, keeps costs down and customers coming back.

Ray Crock, McDonald's founder, created the franchise system that enabled him to not only get other people to finance his vision, but also to get consistent results regardless of who was running an individual restaurant. He created a system and perfected it. This gave him great leverage to grow the business quickly, and he gave franchise owners great freedom to work ON their business and not IN it.

Process Increases Profits

I worked with some highly-skilled brokerage professionals whose business had been growing rapidly. At an executive retreat, they were showing their staff the life cycle of the business to date. Two years before, they were in what we call the "teenage stage." Like a real teenager, this phase is characterized by rapid growth and disdain for rules. Instead, do whatever you must to grow the top line. Go, go, go! This is an exciting time for a company, particularly if it's generating new sales and turning even a modest profit.

It's easy to be fooled into thinking that the teenage stage of a business is productive. In reality, it can be destructive if you're looking for long-term results. Although sales might be up during this phase, profits frequently fall. There's little structure, no process, and even less accountability. For my clients, the absence of a process to monitor market fluctuations was costing them millions and making their company unattractive to investors and prospective clients. Something had to change.

They instituted risk management policies and procedures for the staff to follow. They implemented a training system. They changed their internal climate to foster collaboration among their employees versus competition by changing their compensation plan. Within two years, their business went from one million in losses to five million in profits.

Process Supports Effective Delegation

Recently I sat down with a CEO of a one hundred dollar million company to talk about how I could help him with his time management problem. Constantly late for meetings and repeatedly missing deadlines, Steve felt completely out of control. His family was suffering, and ultimately, he was suffering too.

When we analyzed where he spent his time, we saw that more than half of it was devoted to developing bids and writing proposals. Of course this is very important to obtaining new customers, but I asked if he needed to be involved in all stages of that process. Couldn't someone else do some of it, if not all of it? Frustrated and at the point of breaking down, he said he didn't have the time to train someone who would probably just move on anyway. Like most CEO's, he felt that his business was "different" and more complicated to learn that any other. No wonder he was so involved in each minute aspect of his company.

In truth, it was hard to learn how to perform the steps of developing good proposals, but not because they were so difficult. It was because there was nothing documented. As the saying goes, "nothing documented, nothing gained."

> *If you want something done right, you must document the process.*

As soon as he understood that once his actions were on paper, he could easily train other people and delegate this task to them. He finally saw the light at the end of the tunnel. What's more, he didn't even have to document the process himself (an important point because many people have a hard time documenting their own thoughts and actions). Instead an apprentice would shadow him and write down his thought processes, the questions he asked, and all his steps, transferring what the CEO was doing in order to create a document for other people to follow.

Document Your Actions

The lesson is that when you clearly tell people what the task is and how to do it, your job gets easier! You create freedom and control in how you use your time. The more specific the description, the more consistent the result, and the more freedom you create for yourself. Yes, you have to invest time up front to get the results. But when you think about it strategically, you'll see that this is a wise investment. Which leads to a key observation: Once you convert an activity from an individual action into a process, your team can optimize it. The procedure now becomes something that others cannot only complete on your behalf, but also improve. That's real leverage!

Standards and Optimization: Keeping Process on Track

Now, let's look at the two core components of process: Standards and Optimization. If you aren't managing both of these, your process will fail to yield the best results. For example, have you ever seen a Rube Goldberg machine?

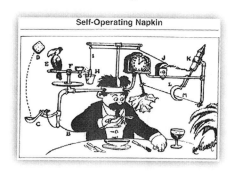

Self-Operating Napkin

They're complicated inventions that purposely employ numerous, convoluted steps to perform what is normally a simple task. They can be a lot of fun for science projects, but you don't want your business to run like one! Utilizing standards and optimization will allow you to cut out the unneeded steps without sacrificing quality or value.

Standards Create Consistency; Consistency Creates Profit

Even if you don't consciously consider them on a regular basis, **standards** are a part of what makes life work. There are standards for your food, your medications, cosmetics, and electronics. There are even industry standards for how your utilities will be delivered to your house, how you will be charged for them, and how the company will contact you.

Standards are all around us, all the time. They affect pretty much every aspect of our lives. Whenever we work with a business, or visit a store, we unconsciously assume that standards are in place.

For example, when you go to a restaurant, you expect a certain standard of cleanliness. It's something you don't think about until you see a napkin on the floor or sit down at a table littered with crumbs. That standard is likely to be a part of the restaurant's process. Somewhere in the back, where customers can't see it, lives a chart outlining what should be cleaned and when. Cleaning standards are essential to an effective process. Without them, your favorite neighborhood bistro would not be able to keep its customers coming back. These standards are applicable from the sales conversation to the final delivery. Every aspect of your business can be standardized to some degree to realize the best possible consistent results.

How to Maintain Standards

Here are some key tools that help you maintain standards to include in defining your processes:

1) **Workflow charts**—Providing a visual overview of the process will make it easier to train and communicate to newcomers in their roles.

2) **Checklists**—Checklists are really useful to hold the person performing the step accountable for covering all the points necessary. And they're also great training tools.

3) **Quality control steps**—Quality control steps should be built into the process to ensure the standards are being followed.

4) **Training**—Make sure all involved are clearly trained so they understand why a particular process matters and how it fits into the big picture. Be sure all know as how to perform their specific functions. Then give them some practice time to demonstrate they understand.

You don't own that standard unless you've documented it clearly. That is why the International Organization for Standardization (ISO) has become an important mechanism to represent quality and best practices. ISO holds those certified to the highest documented standards in their businesses. The challenge in many organizations is getting people to follow the standards effectively and consistently, especially if there is a new implementation. And if those standards aren't followed, they're meaningless and you've wasted your company's time and money developing them.

> *A process that isn't followed isn't worth the paper it's printed on.*

Ultimately, it's the leader's responsibility to motivate and inspire the team to have the incentive and desire to follow standards.

Optimization Increases Productivity

One of the best models of optimization comes from the philosophy of Lean Manufacturing, which defines itself as "the maniacal pursuit of the elimination of waste from every business process with the goal of providing world class quality, delivery, and service to our customers at the lowest possible cost." This philosophy focuses on the process and NOT the people. Lean is about the implementation of the process. It creates a culture that takes the emotion out of the task in order to be more productive.

Everything we do can be improved. Kaizen, the Japanese philosophy of continuously improving business and personal efficiency, literally has no end. It means never-ending improvement. And that starts with exposing and quantifying problems. You need to get to the root cause of the problem, find solutions to implement, and then standardize and create adherence policies and procedures.

For many, the idea of optimization is scary—a terrifying period of expensive consultants, mastering new technologies, manufacturing disruptions, new training, layoffs, and emotional turmoil. Why is that?

"Optimization" Is a Fancy Word for Change

For most people, change is a dirty word. How do you feel about change? How does your team feel about change? Most people experience some sort of fear at the very mention of the word.

Cleaning Up the Process for a Cleaning Company: A Case History

Sara, one of my clients, owns a cleaning business with three locations, many employees, and lots of customers to keep track of. Most of her employees have been with the company for a long time, a point of pride I could hear when she described her low employee turnover. Unfortunately, that pride made it difficult for her to let people go, keeping them even when it was clear that often they weren't a good match for their jobs. She would move around staff positions and create new ones to compensate for the inabilities of a particular person.

> ➤ *Staff doesn't determine process; process determines staff.*

For years, Sara had one manager with inconsistent and unacceptable performance. The manager was in charge of all the cleaners and scheduling. This manager was afraid of change and confrontation, so when she needed to fire a staff member, it didn't happen. Instead, she told Sara that the situation wouldn't happen again. Sara felt like this manager, despite her faults, was loyal, honest, and had the company's best interest at heart. I understood why she wanted to stand by this manager; it's difficult when you feel that an under-performing employee means well. However, no matter what the manager's intentions were, recurring performance issues were being swept under the rug. Sara knew something wasn't right, but she was afraid to find out what it was.

The mistakes and mishaps with this manager were mounting. "She's my right arm," Sara said defensively. "She runs the office and allows me to work on other things. I won't be able to find anyone else to do that for me."

I asked, "If you are operating successfully, why are you losing clients? Why are sales suffering, and employees complaining? If no one ever gets fired for a lack of performance or inappropriate behavior what message does that send to the staff? Do you think that plays a role in the staff's lack of accountability?"

My client went silent. The manager had told her "this office couldn't run without me," and my client chose to accept that as reality. In Sara's mind, her business would fail without this person.

Many business owners feel this way about key staff members. More often than not they are wrong! They often find they have been putting up with subpar performance or accepting behavioral issues at the hand of fear.

➢ *Never be afraid to replace someone who isn't performing.*

Here is what we found as we started to focus more on process and less on people. Sara started re-organizing authority and responsibility. The quality control managers began to take on some of the tasks the manager used to do. This put more checks and balances into place. After the manager took a two-week vacation, it was discovered she had been suppressing client complaints and forging company status reports. She had been doctoring the books to make it look like things were better than they were, which was inconsistent with actual cash flow. It eventually caught up with her.

Once my client investigated and uncovered the lies, she realized she had lost thousands of dollars as a result of her fear. Also, her staff had less respect for her as their leader because she was not making the necessary changes that seemed obvious to everyone but my client.

Of course, after the manager's deceit came to light, Sara let her go. Using the process to define the positions, the reorganization spread the responsibilities across various staff members. Soon, the staff began taking more and more ownership of everything. From quality cleaning, to referrals, to client retention, everything started to move in the right direction.

---◆---

Get People Involved

Winston Churchill said, "Never let a good crisis go to waste," and I couldn't agree more. Periods of change are great opportunities to adjust your team's point of view. These are the times to hold workshops to focus on strategy, communication, leadership, and participation. Going back to strategy and purpose will get everyone connected to the vision and the value creation for the customer. Tell your teams that the goal is to work on process and identify the steps for each task. This will disassociate people from their emotions and focus them on objectives and solutions.

To be successful however, you'll need the involvement and participation of managers and process owners. People support what they create, so get them involved at all levels of change, definition, and implementation. After all, they'll own it after it's implemented. That's one of the biggest failings in consulting: the absence of follow through once the consultants leave. There has to be ownership at all levels, otherwise the new processes or process changes will be short-lived, and the people doing the day-to-day work will quickly revert back to the old methods.

Give Yourself More Freedom

Defining and leveraging your processes gives you confidence as a business owner that things will get done according to the standard you expect. It lowers stress because you know you don't have to be a part of every step of the process. You can take a step back because team members have clarity on how to do their jobs.

A client of mine had a startup that quickly grew to a six-figure business and the stress was mounting with every new client. They were very concerned with doing things at the highest standard, and they weren't sure if it would work to bring others in to support them. Ultimately though, they were unable to perform every task themselves, and I helped them create a process to bring in an expanded workforce to which they could delegate. Just as they completed the process definitions and optimization, the lead partner started to get international clients that required him to travel, and the only way to maintain the existing business was to hire someone to support them immediately. They hired someone who told them that it was the smoothest onboarding process she ever saw. They didn't skip a beat, and the new staff members and doctors could be productive from day one. What a relief!

TAKE AWAYS:

1. Defining your processes creates leverage to grow your business.

2. Build your teams around the processes not the people.

3. Clearly defined processes allow you to delegate effectively and grow your business.

CHAPTER 10: PRIORITIES

Watch out for time vampires

**"The key is not to prioritize what's on your schedule,
but to schedule your priorities."**
- Steven R. Covey

I HAVE A DEAR FRIEND who lives across the country in Seattle. His wedding was the day before a huge presentation that I had to make in Canada. My presentation couldn't be rescheduled, so in order for me even to be at the wedding, I had to leave and fly out before the end of the reception.

As is always the case, there was a long list of odds and ends to finish up in the days right before the presentation. So to arrive at the wedding on time, I had to work on the go. This was a time in my life that I often fell prey to the "one more thing" syndrome. In this case, the extra thing was a presentation handout.

On the day of the wedding, I left my hotel room early to stop by the local Staples to pick up my handouts. I had purposely emailed a layout a few days earlier so that they would be ready in time. My plan was to pick up the presentation handouts before getting ready for the wedding, and then return to my room to dress for the affair. I'd attend the ceremony, handouts and suitcase in my car, spend some time at the reception, and then catch my flight to Canada. I had it all worked out!

Staples, unfortunately was not in on my plan. Their printer had made a mistake and my presentation handouts needed to be rerun. Because I felt like I had to have these handouts, I said I would swing back on the way to the wedding to pick them up. The manager at Staples agreed. "Great! It should only take five minutes to pick them up," I thought.

I had offered to drive two other friends to the wedding from our hotel. When I returned to Staples, a new clerk was working at the printing counter, and there were two people in front of me. I waited and waited. As precious minutes ticked away, I knew I should just leave for the venue. But I was still running that "one more thing" soundtrack in my head. At the last possible second, I rushed out of Staples with my handouts, jumped into my car, and raced ... right into standstill traffic. "Are you kidding me?!" I thought.

I was upset. I mean really upset and embarrassed, because my stubborn desire to cram that last task into an already impossible schedule was now causing my friends to be late, too. If someone had done this to me, I would have been livid.

Just as the wedding procession music started, we raced into the chapel and took our seats. But I was sweating and disgusted with myself. My failure to prioritize what was most important to me nearly prevented me from attending my best friend's wedding ceremony and put innocent bystanders in the same position! I nearly missed the wedding and caused myself a lot of stress that could have easily been avoided.

Let's face it: Those flyers were not as important as our presence at the ceremony. I could have—should have—just left them at Staples. I felt awful about my choices.

That was a hard lesson.

————◆————

Important Things Come First

When you're juggling so much that deadlines are missed and your friends and family suffer, it is time to make a change! Despite the popular conception that being busy is good, being overwhelmed is actually worse than doing nothing! It creates added stress and resistance, the greatest enemies to your productivity. In my friend's wedding example, I wasn't differentiating urgent needs from important needs. The handout seemed urgent to me, and it was. But what was truly important that weekend? The wedding of my close friend was more important, of course. To have true success, important things have to come first.

Remember the Productivity Curve from Chapter 1? I was living my life on the far right-hand side of the curve, so focused on getting things done that I risked compromising the really important stuff, my values. Doing "one more thing" had become an addiction for me, and that's not an exaggeration. Research has shown that when you get something done, it releases the pleasure-inducing chemical dopamine into your system, and it feels good. So you have to make the choice to break that habit. Priorities pave the way peak levels of execution and satisfaction.

> *Setting clear priorities plays a major role in keeping you in the Productivity Zone.*

There are two different types of priorities: Short-Term and Long-Term. In the same way that you have short and long-term goals, you will have priorities that reflect them. Priorities are highly individualized, and while two people might have the same goal, it's unlikely they'll have the same priorities driving them towards that goal. That's because your priorities are also expressions of your values and your strategies or way of achieving them.

To Do or Not to Do

The more your goals represent your values, strengths, and passions, the more likely you are to achieve them. They represent what is important to you and to your business. When you set your priorities based upon what is important to you, your progress in these areas is what makes you feel productive and in the Productivity Zone. An overarching theme that I'll come back to again and again is Importance vs. Urgency. Steven R. Covey, the author of *7 HABITS OF HIGHLY EFFECTIVE PEOPLE*, first came up with this concept to illustrate how priorities can return us to our values. Championship Psychology provides you with the components and strategies you need to consistently align your priorities and your values.

Don't Should on Yourself

I have clients who get so caught up in what they think is urgent that their truly important projects and tasks, the ones that got them into this business in the first place, are neglected. They live completely in reaction mode. A lot of people are stuck with to-do lists that have vague "shoulds" rather than clearly expressed priorities. More important than your to-do list is your top three list of priorities for the day. Having clarity about your top priorities is what will keep you focused on what is important. Your priorities affect everything else you do. So, the question is, when is the last time you evaluated how you set your priorities?

There are three key components of setting clear priorities: Values, Importance, and Delegation.

VALUES

Our **values** are the thoughts and beliefs that are integral to who we are. They shape our behavior, our passions, our sense of right and wrong. Consider our earlier discussion of rules and boundaries from the chapter on language. Values are boundaries that we apply to ourselves rather than others. However, just as we sometimes engage in unhealthy relationships with people who are not meeting our needs, we often neglect our own values! This affects our trust in others and, worse than that, our trust in ourselves.

Maybe honesty is an important value to you, but you find yourself lying occasionally to avoid conflict. Maybe health is a critical part of your self-definition, but you find yourself eating fast food regularly just to fit in a meal.

Let's look at a few ways that your values may not be congruent with your actions:

Align Your Needs and Values

Here's a big secret many of us don't realize, and those who do don't want to admit: We humans will always do things that meet our needs. If you're hungry you will find food. And the hungrier you become, the more you'll be willing to sacrifice something else to get that food. Sometimes there are "easy" ways of meeting our needs that may not align with our values. It's very difficult to walk away from these influences.

> ➤ *When we are out of alignment with our values it produces undesirable and unproductive emotions.*

If you feel sluggish or unhappy or unproductive, examine how your needs are being met. It's possible that you're living out of alignment without realizing it.

Our Self-Definition Does Not Match Our Desires

Possibly from past experiences, we have created limiting beliefs that have shaded the way we see and define ourselves. The end result is we don't always believe we are capable or worthy of what we want. This lack of cohesiveness between our beliefs and our desires takes us away from our values. By now, you probably can see the underlying influence that our Championship Psychology has on us. Simply setting priorities but procrastinating is a form of self-sabotage.

When we're out of alignment with our values, our priorities get skewed. "Quick and easy" becomes more important than "something done right." Over time your personal and professional relationships will suffer as a result.

Make a list of your values, how you define them, and how you intend to live by them. This creates something concrete to hold you accountable to living in alignment. Make sure you order these values to be clear which ones come first. If Integrity is before Loyalty, the results will be very different than the other way around if both are challenged at the same time.

IMPORTANCE

As I said earlier, many of us fall prey to a false sense of urgency. When we create urgency around tasks that don't warrant it, we take valuable energy and resources away from the truly important tasks. We get busy with purposeless activity. These are our time vampires. Almost all of my clients who reported feeling overwhelmed and overloaded were operating with a false sense of urgency. Low priority tasks were treated as essential, while the important tasks never got done, and the to-do list kept growing and growing and growing.

As the business owner, you should be focusing on important, not urgent matters. You are probably thinking, "Well if I don't do the urgent stuff, who will? Everything else will fail." Will it? Are these tasks really urgent? Most of us make things urgent when they are not. Or we create these urgencies from our lack of planning and spending time on what's NOT important. That, by the way, is procrastination, even though we don't like to see it that way in the moment.

The first question to ask is, "Who else could do this?" Urgent tasks are why you have a team. Creating a strategic plan for a new expansion to your business is important. Paying the electric bill is urgent.

Urgency Has a Price

It was a call to action. The CEO of an IT services organization came to me with an urgent request. John, the Head of

Operations, had worked himself into such a frenzy trying to satisfy everyone at every moment that he wound up in the hospital on an extended sick leave.

"Penny," the CEO said. "If you don't make progress in helping John with his time management issues, he won't get the raise he is looking for at the beginning of the year. I need him to set an example for his team. I am giving him this chance to work with you, and I really hope you can help him."

I spoke with John on the phone for our first session and asked him to describe his typical day to me. As John rattled off the various projects that he was simultaneously responsible for on a daily basis, it became clear to me that there was no way one person could actually accomplish all his responsibilities in a timely manner. Not only did he manage operations, but he also had client responsibilities, which could take up to seventy percent of his time.

This is not unusual of small growing businesses, but in addition to that, the CEO had "special projects" for him on a regular basis. And—if you can imagine this—his desk sat right in the middle of a large open room where he was constantly interrupted with staff needing direction and reinforcement. On weeknights he would regularly work until six or seven pm, and then go home for a few hours to see his kids before returning to work three or four more hours. Weekends involved a few hours of work here and there as well. There was hardly any time at all for John. No wonder he felt like he couldn't breathe!

"John," I asked him, "when your boss comes to you with special projects what do you say?"

"What can I say?" he glumly replied. "He's the CEO, so I take it and do it."

I pressed a little further. "What about when a client sets a deadline for you? What do you do?"

Again he said, "The client is king, so I do everything within my power to make that deadline."

Evaluating John's methodology was simple: When people asked him to jump, his question was "how high?" Clearly this is not the best response under these circumstances.

———◆———

Quality Questions Help You to Be More Strategic

You learned in the earlier sections of this book that the quality of our questions makes all the difference in the quality of our success. Asking new questions helped John get out of the cycle where everything on his plate was critical and required immediate attention. With every new task, he started to ask a few questions:

- Is this urgent?
- What is the flexibility on the due date?
- Could a part of this be done by that date to satisfy an immediate need, and then the rest be broken into smaller milestones for future deadlines?
- Will this task bring him closer to his goals?
- What results really need to be achieved?
- Is that result really worth **his** time and energy?

These simple questions gave him flexibility to address the expectations of the people around him, including his staff. Most important, John learned to say NO to his boss. And, guess what? It didn't get him in trouble; in fact, his boss recognized that John was successfully self-managing and became more confident in John's abilities to get the job done.

Now It's Your Turn

I'd like you to imagine at the end of each day connecting to what's really important to you and your greater purpose. Visualize yourself already having achieved it and how great it feels and how things will be different now that you've reached those goals. How much more focus would you have? Make a point to spend the first hour or two in the morning focusing on something that advances you towards those ultimate goals that you've set for yourself, even if that means going to bed earlier so you can get up earlier!

> ➢ *You'll still have 1,320 minutes left in the day to do whatever's urgent.*

Also, make sure your environment is set up to support you. To eliminate distractions, get the biggest items done first. With a little planning, you'll have less urgency. Identify your critical success factors and set your priorities around them. It can be difficult to distinguish what's important from what's urgent—especially since many of us are taught from an early age to place urgency on low priority tasks.

Here's a simple tip to help you separate the urgent from the important: Don't just ask yourself what's critical. Question anyone else involved in setting these goals and these deadlines.

I once worked with an organizer who would help people decide what to keep in their offices and what to box up. She was merciless, but effective! Her secret was to have them look at each item that was cluttering the room and ask three questions: "Do I need it? Do I love it? Does it make me money?"

I suggest to you today that you can approach your life and task list in the exact same way. Things that you need include tasks like paying the electric bill, or buying paper for the printer, or doing the grocery shopping. Things that you love are the tasks that brings you joy and fulfillment and give you energy so that you can be better focused and appreciate what you achieve more. And the tasks that result in financial gain should be obvious. Once you eliminate all the low-priority errands, chores and time wasters that don't fit into those categories, you'll be amazed at the results.

DELEGATION

One common trait of the mega-successful is that they delegate. Delegation, ladies and gentlemen, is the millionaire mindset. If in doubt, delete and delegate. Successful people know where their strengths are, and they don't waste precious time doing things outside their skill set. Instead, they leverage the strengths of others. They know how to ask great questions and how to allow someone else have the answers. That's freedom! Essentially, they've learned to focus on their goals and objectives and not solely on the activities.

> *The #1 way of avoiding stress and overload is to enlist the support of others.*

Think of it this way. You CAN actually buy time with delegation. Doing everything yourself is impossible and improbable, so at the end of the day, there is no one to blame—except you.

YOU CAN
DO ANYTHING,
BUT NOT
EVERYTHING.

—David Allen

In 2014, a Time Management and Productivity Study conducted by the FPA Research and Practice Institute found that "sixty-eight percent of managers would like to increase their use of delegation as a time management and personal development tool." So why don't they? And more importantly, *why don't you?* Many people are concerned with the upfront time it might take to get started, and they feel that it's just faster to do it themselves. If you're one of those people, here's my question: How's that been working for you so far? Maybe you can do it faster, but have you considered what your time is worth?

Do you run around to find the best deals? To what extent will you go to save money? All of us know someone who will drive twenty miles to save a few cents on gas. He loves the game and the win, but is he really winning when he spends a few hours of his time to save a few bucks? Don't be that guy!

He obviously isn't clear what his time is worth, and you need to know the value of your time, too. You need to be connected to what else you could be doing with that time. Let's look at it rationally. Let's say you make one hundred dollars per hour. Every time you go twenty minutes out of your way it's essentially costing you thirty-three dollars in lost time. When you feel that urge to go far out of your way for a deal, look at the time in terms of money, and then decide if it's really worth it. If it's an activity you enjoy, you might be spending your time well. But does it make sense to spend thirty-three dollars to save two fifty in gas? Of course not! So start valuing yourself right now!

Often we have a mindset that pricing determines value. When estimating your time, take into account the unique value of your time! Go to www.p10app.com/bookresources to better understand what your time is really worth.

Ultimately, you're looking for peak performance. I know you have achieved a great deal of success in your life already, but allow me to add some perspective. Think of yourself as a racecar driver who's made it to the big track. Would you still change your own tires during a race? Knowing what's at stake at these speeds, do you want a cheap mechanic, or someone who you know you can count on to get the job done, and get it done right? You want the best person for the job. Why jeopardize your place in the race by wasting time and taking risks on the cheap? We've already discussed the importance of a Championship Team, and you'll really see the payoff of that when it's time to delegate. If you want to perform at your best, surround yourself with the best, and let them do their best for you!

TAKE AWAYS:

1. Urgent matters are not always important and will usually not advance your growth.

2. Everything can't be a priority or you create stress, overwhelm and disappointment.

3. Ask better questions to get clear on your priorities.

4. Delegation is a strength and enables growth.

CHAPTER 11: SUSTAINABLE RESULTS

"Effective leadership is not about making speeches or being liked; leadership is defined by results not attributes."

- Peter Drucker

Recognize the Specifics of Your Success

"ONCE I HAVE ENOUGH CREDIBILITY, I plan to bring this program to other practitioners," my new client confided. I see this so often. Fear holds people back from taking that next step—the BIG STEP that will take them outside of their comfort zone. They get to a point and distort, delete, and generalize their success. This means they fail to recognize the success they have already achieved. Often this is a protection mechanism to stay where they are comfortable and follow the path of least resistance because that is what their brains look for.

"How many people have successfully been cured in your program—ten or twenty?" I asked, knowing full well the numbers were much higher.

"No," he said, "thousands."

"Oh!" I acted surprised. "So what does enough credibility look like?" I prodded him further. "Who decides when you have enough?"

I could see his face shift as he answered these questions in his head; he was realizing he was putting these barriers on his ability to take his business to the next level.

"If I were a patient looking for a cure," I said, "and you had thousands of people you helped to overcome their illness without medication, that would be enough for me to engage in the program." Then I reminded him of something Tony Robbins did early in his career when the public did not have much awareness of his abilities to help people make major transformations. He made a challenge on a TV program and said, "Bring me the toughest unsolvable cases and I will transform them." He built instant credibility overnight when he transformed these difficult cases on public TV.

I could see the final shift in my new client's face, the anxiety fell away, and the options started to open up in his mind. "What do you think is your next step?" I asked, curious to learn what had changed. He was ready to recognize his current successes, look at the specifics of his progress, and define his next steps to bring his concept to other practitioners!

By not recognizing and measuring the specifics of your achievements, you may be holding yourself back from fueling your next move. Self-reflection enables you to see clearly your path going forward and to take more proactive measures to ensure maintainable results.

———◆———

We have discussed the principles and 10 Core Drivers of Championship Psychology and Winning Strategies. So where is this leading you? Why put in the time and energy to change the way you think, to create new habits and rituals, and incorporate these principles fully into your life?

To Create Even Better Results and Get in the Productivity Zone!

Now, what if I told you that you can have not only better results, but also self-sustaining ones?! You want outcomes that you can consistently achieve every time, ideally with less effort. When you attain this level of repeated, tried-and-true progress, your business can run without you! You can take that vacation that you haven't taken in years. Go ahead. Go to the beach with your family, knowing that your office will run as if you were there. If you hear yourself saying, "That sounds great, and that works for others but not for me," revisit the first section of the book because you still need some work on your Championship Psychology! If you know it is possible and want to know how . . . keep reading.

The Final Blade

Sustainable Results are the final blade of your productivity windmill, and this blade is made up of **Progress, Measurement** and **Proactivity.** These are the final elements in fully transforming your life, outlook, and results. To create this you need to have standards and systems that are documented so they can be communicated, measured, and optimized. You want to analyze current and future situations proactively so as to adapt with flexibility, staying ahead of the curve and in the productivity zone. I've said this before: Each element builds upon the one before; there is a sequence. In order to create sustainable dramatic growth, you must start at the beginning with your Championship Psychology; only then can you master Winning Strategies. The same is true of Sustainable Results. Before we move on to the last three elements, let's review what we've learned so far.

Your New Mantra

My college professor used to say, "If you want your students to hear you, you have to say it three times." So, before we go any further, I want to reiterate the 7 Principles of a Championship Psychology. Make these your mantra. Challenge yourself to repeat and review them every morning and every night. When they become a fundamental part of who you are, you'll begin to feel real success. I tell my clients all the time, "It's not about what you do, its about how you feel about what you did." If you want to change your results, you need to change how you feel. Productivity is as much a feeling as it is about what you are actually achieving.

> ➤ *To change how you feel you have to change how you think, and what you think about.*

Let's review the seven presuppositions of a Championship Psychology:

- **You create your own identity**—As children we often take on definitions and labels from others; the truth is you decide who you are and who you will become.

- **Choice is your greatest gift**—You can't choose all of the events you will experience, but you can choose the meaning you give any event.

- **Energy is everything**—How we manage our energy will determine the meaning and quality of results we receive.

- **Ask quality questions**—To get a better answer, ask a better question.

- **What is learned can be unlearned**—All behavior is learned. If a behavior of yours is not serving your goals, replace it with a new one that will move you along the path you want to be on.

- **No failure, only feedback**—It is okay to feel negative emotions, but don't live there; learn from them and move on.

- **Environment is paramount**—Instead of trying to push past the place you are in, be in a better place!

As we move into the chapters on Sustainable Results, I want you to reflect on those bullet points. How can you apply these in your life and within your team at work? You can lead by example. Energy Management starts with your personal energy, which will impact, influence and change your teams environment and energy too.

Teach your team the 10 Core Drivers of productivity and then help to create a supportive and accountable environment. Most companies hold meetings about sales strategies, implementation, and sales challenges on a weekly basis to measure bottom line results. It's time well spent. Imagine the results when you spend time with your team also focusing on productivity strategies, implementation, and personal productivity challenges. Remember, productivity equals profits. Great leadership is focusing your time and energy on resolving what's holding your team back: remove the obstacles and look out!

Think about it. You are in control. In order to create sustainable growth for your business, you need to know and verify what works and under what conditions. This is the same for any area of your life. It's one thing to make a change and have good results, but unless you compare them to what you've previously achieved, you don't really know if you have progress. I have worked with clients who felt like they knew their sales closure rate. When we actually started to physically track it, they were surprised how low the rate was. It was half of what they expected it to be. You can't ignore the data. Trust me—you need the data. When you have data, you can see the difference between progress and just simply change.

We live in a world of change, and although we're creatures of habit, the key to our success (survival of the fittest) is to adapt. If we want to do more than just survive and start to really thrive, proactivity makes all the difference. This is where we heighten our flexibility due to the ability to anticipate changes and come up with calculated or strategic options. This is where preparation meets anticipation.

CHAPTER 12: PROGRESS

"The beatings will continue until morale improves"

"People may take a job for more money, but they often leave it for more recognition and appreciation."
- Bob Nelson

Feeling Productive

I WAS WORKING WITH A client who, more often than not, would finish her days frustrated that she was not productive. She would beat herself up about what she should have been doing or could have been doing. She was focused on what she didn't get done—not on what she had actually accomplished. This was a reoccurring theme for her, a mindset that often led her to the far sides of the productivity curve. It reduced her to procrastination and apathy, so she could continually be hard on herself—or get stuck in the anxiousness of the "just one more thing" side of perfectionism in an attempt to reduce her to-do list. After we talked about her mental focus and looked at her language, her face lit up as she said to me, "So a better question to ask is, "Where and how was I productive today?"

"Yes," I said, pleased she had made this connection. "What progress did I make today and/or what did I learn to help me progress tomorrow?" I told her as long as she was making headway in some shape or form, she would FEEL satisfied and useful. Her new daily assignment was to focus on what she accomplished versus what she did not. It's amazing what a shift in perspective can do for you.

———◆———

You can see how intertwined our psychology is with each of the key drivers of our productivity. Go back to the Championship Psychology principle, "there is no failure, only feedback." Recognizing our progress allows us to create even more momentum. When we have a Championship Psychology, we have the foundation we need to create Sustainable Results because our Championship psychology is intertwined in all of the 10 Core Drivers.

It Isn't What You Think

When you see progress, you often have a better view of your potential and a better outlook to stay consistent and committed. So progress matters in a number of ways. Fundamentally, the way to increase the frequency of a behavior is to reward it. The way to acknowledge progress is to reward behavior with acknowledgement, celebration, and the implementation of resources needed to keep replicating and building on that success.

As we saw with my client above, most people incorrectly define progress. They think it is simply the act of achievement. But actually, progress is about gaining traction. And traction is not only realized through direct achievement, it's also realized through learning and understanding.

> *It means having the ability to push forward.*

If the tires on your car don't have traction, the car won't move forward. You might even slide backwards! You ensure your car will have traction by maintaining the tires. If a tire is worn, or not working correctly, you'd repair or replace it. The same should be true of your business practices. If you aren't getting traction and moving forward, then you know you need to diagnose the issue and correct it. Just knowing that there is a problem and taking steps to rectify it is its own kind of progress!

Building on the presupposition that "there is no failure, only feedback," we can appreciate that progress is not always successfully achieving something. Rather, it is any time we can take a situation and gain from it. When we learn something, we have the ability to grow. I say the "ability" as we haven't really grown until we have applied what we've learned. That is the principle of progress. Change is a natural function of time. If you do nothing things will change; however, this does not necessarily equate to advancement or improvement. There are three fundamental elements of progress: **Learning, Recognition,** and **Celebration.**

LEARNING IS PROGRESS

An important concept to internalize is that learning is synonymous with progress. That means any situation can create growth no matter the results, as long as you learn from the experience. Learning is not only recognizing what went right or wrong, but also applying that knowledge to avoid a similar situation in the future.

Do you remember the section on focus? Where you place your attention in the moment will determine the level of productivity and progress you're capable of making. Be mindful of the "Now," but make sure to schedule time to reflect on the past (what you've learned), and to prepare for the future. This is what learning is really about: Use each situation as an opportunity to grow.

Think about the implications of the word "progress." Most people would associate it with societal growth and advancement. Someone who is on the cutting edge of technology or culture might be described as "progressive." This is because, at its core, progress is about positive change, and that can't happen without learning. We can choose to make every situation positive, thereby increasing our traction and enabling ourselves to maximize our potential. Or, we can choose to keep creating negative beliefs around results that didn't come out in our favor, thereby limiting our potential.

There Is No Failure, Only Feedback

One of my mentors, Steve Linder, founder of Neuro-Strategies, recommends that you ask yourself four questions any time you get a result that you didn't want. They'll help you reinforce the belief that all feedback is positive. Remember, any result is just information. It's what you do with the information that counts.

Four Questions for Growth

- **What does this outcome mean?** Ask that question a few times to get a few different perspectives about what this result could mean. The first response is usually your Automatic Negative Thought (ANT) so keep asking to get beyond that.
- **What can I learn from this?** It has to be positive and something for which you can take responsibility. Understand your role and what you can do differently.
- **How can you apply this in the future?** What specific actions can you take next time to get the result you want?
- **How can you share this?** When we share something, we learn it acts as a multiplier and reinforces the learning and application. We own it.

Another way to think of the four questions is in the framework of the children's game Hotter/Colder. What happens when you stand in the center of the room and take no action? Nothing! No progress or regression. It's only when you move in one direction that you start to get feedback and adjust accordingly. Even if the response is that "you're getting colder," it gives you the opportunity to correct your direction.

RECOGNITION ENHANCES ENGAGEMENT

A 2013 Gallup poll found that only thirteen percent of employees are engaged in their work. Only thirteen percent! Why? Perhaps a large portion of the other eighty-seven percent feel as though they're not being recognized for their contributions. Recognition is the act of increasing engagement and productivity through communication, reward, and satisfaction. And that's not only in the workplace, but also in *every aspect of your life.* Science tells us that when we achieve something and are recognized for that achievement, it affects us physiologically. Our system releases serotonin, and if that positive response continues to occur, our neurological chemistry actually changes over time! When you earn praise in the form of a ceremony, status, or public celebration, it evokes a feeling of happiness, pride, and self-confidence, and it increases the desire to continue to add worth and be appreciated in this way. In addition, we create the high-quality energy needed to see championship results.

In Championship Psychology, we discussed that one of the greatest drivers in our psychology is the value we feel that we bring to others, or in other words, our contribution. The best teams rely on each member bringing different strengths to the team to complement one another.

➢ *Acknowledging the contributions of your team (and yourself!) builds trust.*

In Steven M. R. Covey's book, *THE SPEED OF TRUST*, he writes that creating trust is the fastest way to increase productivity. Attributing merit to yourself and others has great power, an important foundation for building a thriving culture and positive work environment with Sustainable Results!

Let's consider some statistics from a 2013 Badgeville study that polled the value and importance of recognition in the workplace across various industries:

- **Celebrations:** Ninety percent of respondents said that a fun work environment is very or extremely motivating. This means celebrating anniversaries, birthdays, personal events (like weddings), and milestones. Just recognizing the consistent application of standards can make a huge difference in your employee's drive to keep performing at that standard. Celebrating your accomplishments is a part of keeping that traction that moves you forward. That is what keeps the car oiled and working optimally. After all, what was the point of all the work and energy if you aren't going to appreciate what you've achieved?

- **Verbal:** Eighty percent of employees said recognition for contributions is more fulfilling than any rewards and gifts. Offer compliments in the moment, just when you catch someone doing something right! You don't have to save them for year-end reviews. Those small unplanned kudos go a long way. Remember to be relevant, specific, descriptive, and measured. Enable your staff, friends and family to see their worth and really own it. Always be authentic; remember sixty-five percent of our communication is nonverbal. If your face and body language aren't congruent with your message, you will come across as insincere—and destroy the goodwill you hoped to establish.

- **Monetary:** Seventy-one percent interviewed said the most meaningful recognition they received had no dollar value. Money and bonuses are important, but many employers focus rewards solely on raises or bonuses. Most of the time, these do not represent large sums of money. Believe it or not, the average employee will gain more from a workplace celebration than a five-cent raise.
- **Experiential:** Create an experience to share with the team or for yourself. The top reasons people stay in organizations are: 1) working with people they like, and 2) opportunities for growth. Experiences enhance relationships. This can mean anything from a weekend-long company retreat to taking the team out for lunch. Those outside-the-workplace connections cannot be manufactured in your office.

➤ *Recognition should match effort and results or it loses meaning.*

It isn't the activity that matters as much as the feeling that comes of it.

> *"People won't remember what you said, but they will remember how you made them feel."*
>
> - Maya Angelou

You should acknowledge your team and yourself though ACTIVE recognition. An example of this is an Employee-of-the-Month plaque. It's a visual reminder that your work isn't going unnoticed!

CELEBRATION

In my experience, the "celebration muscle" is woefully underused. Some people have a real problem with stopping and appreciating their own progress and that of the people they manage or even love. The reasons range from "I don't have time for it" to "I don't deserve it." Some people aren't even aware of their own growth. A great example of this was the story at the beginning of the section on Sustainable Results. When he discounted the hundreds of cures he had achieved, he was just outright deleting all the great results he has achieved to date. When we process information, activities, and events, we filter them to give them meaning. Often we delete, distort, and generalize to make ourselves right.

Several studies have shown that the most effective way to create permanent habits is through positive reinforcement. So you're actually doing yourself a favor, and are more likely to **reach your goals sooner**, by celebrating.

Here again is a physiological impact that results from achieving milestones or being rewarded by others. As we said earlier, our brains release dopamine every time we achieve something we set out to do. But here's the secret sauce: Over time, your brain becomes accustomed to that dopamine level and releases oxytocin. This means that when you recognize your successes, it actually changes your brain chemistry! If you've ever wondered why some people seem happy all the time, this is it. Their brains are conditioned to be happy, and yours could be too!

Have you heard the old adage "you'll catch more flies with honey than vinegar"? You can apply this to yourself. Setting small short-term rewards to celebrate your success will keep you pushing forward. These rewards do not have to be extravagant. Maybe it's as small as getting your nails done, or having lunch at a restaurant you like. Whenever my assistant and I meet an important business goal, I take us out for massages. We'll take the afternoon off to focus on health and happiness and acknowledge what we've accomplished together. I often involve her in the planning of our festivities. During our meetings I will say, "Megan, when we reach this goal, how will we celebrate?" By involving her in the process, she looks forward to it more. Encourage your employees to weigh in on how best to observe their accomplishments. They will respect you as a leader for caring about them and for making sure they're happy in their jobs. Similarly, reward yourself with what makes you happy, and you'll find that the fire, passion, and energy to keep getting things done will burn much hotter!

TAKE AWAYS:

1. There is no failure, only feedback.

2. The opportunity to learn something increases your potential.

3. Recognizing progress creates traction and further engagement.

CHAPTER 13: MEASUREMENT

Analysis Paralysis

"You can't manage what you don't measure"
- W. Edwards Deming

SUSAN LOOKED AT THE NUMBERS again. Shaking her head in frustration, she mumbled to herself that they were still down. She would bring them to the Monday meeting and show her team. They needed to see that they were lagging. Hopefully, they could offer some explanation as to why.

"I don't understand," she told me. "We won the regional award for reaching these sales targets two years ago, so I know they are possible. Now the staff just doesn't seem to care."

"How often do you review the numbers with them?" I asked.

"Every week," she said with a sigh.

"How often do you review the numbers?" I probed a bit further.

"Twice a day." she said frustrated.

"I see. What are you measuring every week?" I pursued.

She gave me the usual—sales, expense ratios, etc.

"Do your employees have a part of setting these goals?" I queried further.

"No," she said. "I give them the numbers based on last year and the sales figures provided by corporate."

I thought I found the problem. "If they have no understanding of how these numbers came to be, perhaps they feel they don't have an influence on them. Is that possible?" I asked, trying to lead her to the core of her issue. "Perhaps you looking at them twice a day is increasing your frustration," I continued. "This way doesn't seem to be working and it's causing you a great deal of stress. Are you open to working with a new way?"

"Yes," she said, eager to turn things around.

"Ask your people what they believe are the drivers of the sales figures, and brainstorm about the obstacles that are preventing them from increasing these values."

She was willing to give it a try. Susan changed the format of her Monday meeting to weekly workshops. They created action plans to move those business drivers, or lead indicators. This had a domino effect of changes for the organization. Instead of being frozen and incapable of finding real solutions, her team was motivated and became involved in creating better systems and processes to ensure better quality and customer service. There were new incentives, which brought even greater engagement and satisfaction to the team. Susan's whole organizational structure improved. Best of all, Susan let go of a lot of frustration from over-analyzing the factors that didn't drive the business. She was able to take more time off while her employees ran the show. At the same time, her sales, profits and loyalty figures grew. In one year's time, she was back to leading her division sales.

———◆———

The moral of this story is that the problem usually isn't what you see at the surface. What people perceive to be the problem often is not the core issue. Much of their time and energy is going into the symptoms of the core problem and only act as a temporary bandage. For example, firing someone for not meeting the numbers doesn't really resolve anything (don't get me wrong, sometimes it's necessary, but you may find that isn't the solution). Let's look at how measurement can be used to get to the root cause of what ails your business.

Selecting what to measure is as important, if not more important, as the measurement itself. Many people get caught up in the metrics and lose sight of the big picture. Too often I see clients evaluating a preconceived problem instead of analyzing what the problem actually is! When you're clear on your expected outcome, and measure the right things, you can effectively and consistently monitor key performance indicators and the important drivers.

➤ *What most people perceive to be the problem often is NOT the core issue.*

It's WHAT You Measure That Matters Most!

Effective measurement is made up of three essential elements: **Accountability**, **GAPS**, and **Key Drivers**.

ACCOUNTABILITY

The way people react to the word accountability, you'd think it was an obscenity! Many people recoil at the very mention of it. This concept seems to have a negative connotation. Often people say it when they're speaking about results that were NOT achieved. It's often viewed as a consequence for poor performance, punishment executed upon you to ensure that you comply the next time around.

Ownership Makes People Accountable

Listen to your tone of voice as you say out loud: "to hold someone accountable." Chances are it sounded harsh. Probably not very motivating either. So I want you to let go of the idea that accountability is something that happens only after a problem. It's not about taking blame, it's about taking ownership, and it starts in the beginning of the process. This type of true accountability is developed through two areas: purpose and engagement.

First, purpose comes from the person's connection to the value received for them and the receiver, the client for instance. We talked about purpose in Chapter 3. Ownership is where desire is created and you get connected to the underlying reason you want to do something. The other three elements of Championship Psychology and Winning Strategies reinforce and support purpose and ownership. You don't measure for accountability; you measure to manage and optimize strategy.

To create desire, build ownership, and tap into people's motivation, they have to understand it from their own perspective. They need to be aligned with the organizational values. Involve your team in goal setting, creating strategies, planning, and setting priorities wherever possible. Remember— people support what they create. They are connected to the purpose and provide engagement. If you have an issue with accountability with yourself or others, you have a lack of ownership. You need to go back to the section on Championship Psychology. The truth is that a lack of accountability in staff is not necessarily an employee issue; it could very well be a leadership issue.

Here are three simple ways to increase ownership and accountability:

Workshops: There's no better engagement tool than a workshop. They can be fast, fun, and an effective way to involve everyone in the group. Workshops create contribution, collaboration, and consensus. They also offer a great forum for collecting new ideas. The key is to make sure you establish a process to follow-up on communication and implementation; otherwise, people may feel they're not being heard.

Encourage a culture of learning: Review the results after a project, reporting period, or situation. Meet together to identify what you all learned. What were factors that contributed to success, and what were the resistance factors that prevented it? Then create an action plan of how your learned concepts will be applied.

Reward and celebrate: People want to be appreciated and recognized for their contribution. We often hear the best way to raise kids and train dogs are with positive recognition. Adults are no different. When we reward the behavior, we want to see we will get more of it. This goes for your team, your relationships, and yourself.

Susan's story at the beginning of this chapter demonstrated the benefits of shifting your mindset to change the way you look at accountability. Susan approached her staff about accountability and she shifted the culture of the organization by shifting her leadership style to engage rather than command. It works!

GAPS

Measurement means finding an effective and sustainable way of identifying where you currently are relative to where you want to be. It's the part of your journey where you stop to check your map to see how far you've traveled and if you're going in the right direction. When I work with clients, the first thing we do is a GAP analysis. First, we get a clear understanding of their goals and objectives. Then we pinpoint where they are now so that we can accurately assess the gap. If you don't know where you are, you have no baseline to evaluate growth and to demonstrate progress. It seems obvious but so many people don't do this.

Where Are You Now?

Consider your baseline and benchmarks on your map. When you're driving and get lost, what's the first thing you look for on a map? It's where you are now. That's your baseline, or point of comparison moving forward.

> *You won't be able to chart a course to your destination if you don't know where you are now.*

All achievement—or the lack of it—is measured by how far you've gone from that point.

Know Where You Are Going

The benchmark is the point of destination. Measuring the distance between where you are now and your destination helps you decide on a path and clarifies what it takes to get to the next place of comparison.

Benchmarks are important to our success and sustainability. They mark the measurement of each step of the process. So that is why we track the number of sales calls and compare that with how many appointments were generated. They're a means and range for comparison. They enable you to identify areas for improvement and optimize growth.

Some companies provide benchmark information for industries to be able to compare your operations and sales ratios to others in your industry. I have a client who has actively started to use industry measurements to provide greater clarity on their efficiency and effectiveness. It helps push their management team to meet the goal to be top in their industry.

Measure Your Personal Productivity

My unique program, the P10: Productivity Accelerator Assessment was created for this purpose. How can we manage our time and energy if we don't know what specifically it's made up of in order to create a baseline to measure it against? We need to specify the criteria. Not utilizing a tool like the Productivity Accelerator Assessment is one of the reasons we experience less consistency in our behavior. We aren't measuring personal productivity based on the 10 Core Drivers, giving it the type of focus and attention it needs. By measuring the right criteria we align all of our resources to to figure out how to close the GAP.

KEY DRIVERS

When it comes to measurement, what really matters is WHAT you're measuring. If you focus your energy on measuring the wrong things, the best you can hope for is to stand still, and more likely it will actually move you away from your goal! All too often, when my clients aren't seeing growth and prosperity, I find that they were measuring lag indicators. On the other hand, when I find a business that is growing and thriving, I can guarantee you they are measuring lead indicators, which are the business drivers that, when measured on a regular basis, can warn us of a flaw in the design and enable us to adapt and adjust before it is too late.

Lag Indicators: This is when you measure the same results over and over again. Let's say sales are down. They've been down for three months now. Each month, you measure your sales and discover what you already knew. Unfortunately, this doesn't help you. By evaluating concrete sales results you're focusing on what isn't working. Often when the numbers are not being met, companies use accountability as a consequence versus a driver. Instead of putting out the fire, it tends to add fuel and creates a dissatisfied staff and management team, which eventually leads to apathy.

Lead Indicators: These are indicators that focus on trends. If lag indicators are about counting results, lead indicators are about predicting them. Rather than measuring actual sales, you measure leads and referrals and the activities that get you the sales results you're targeting. Lead indicators are what generate growth. If your leads and referrals are down, that may tell you that you need to focus energy and resources on marketing. If leads are up, but your team isn't closing sales, you may need to concentrate on training. Lead indicators give you information you can really use to implement change.

Imagine that you're a contractor building a house. The mantra you live by is "measure twice, cut once." But you don't have to be a contractor to benefit from the concept. Apply that mentality to any aspect of your life and business:

- Measurement allows you to see where you are on the road to success and avoid time and costly investments on paths that aren't moving you forward.
- Measurement provides feedback.
- Measurement tells you when and where you need more or fewer resources on a project. It tells you if you've come any closer to your overall goals, or if you are stuck in place and need a new course of action.

Progress is about celebrating what you've done, and then recognizing and learning from where you have fallen short. Measuring your results is about reflecting on them, looking for patterns, and identifying where and how to take action. If you aren't evaluating your business appropriately, you aren't effectively managing. Take charge now!

TAKE AWAYS:

1. Accountability is more about ownership than poor results.

2. Measurement is the best way to learn what works and what needs adjustment.

3. Be clear on what are the drivers of your business.

4. Know your baselines and benchmarks against which to measure.

CHAPTER 14: PROACTIVITY

There are better ways
to anticipate the
future of your company

"A leadership culture is one where everyone thinks like
an owner, a CEO or a managing director. It's one
where everyone is entrepreneurial and proactive."
- Robin Sharma

"WE WON!" I EXCLAIMED, DOING a little happy dance.
The members of my team looked at me as if I had
lost my mind. "But we came in second," someone said.

"Yes," I replied, "the award for Best Utility shows that we
came in as runner-up. But we won because we got the publicity
and the awareness we wanted to get."

Don't get me wrong; I would have liked to earn first place, but in this case, winning the award wasn't the goal. The real objective was to create greater awareness in the public about using our company's technology.

"All of this puts us in a great place to start talking to companies about buying us out."

"Buying us out?" Laura from my team asked, "Why would we want to sell now when things are really starting to gain traction?"

She was right. We had built this business over four years into a multi-million dollar company. But what she didn't understand was that when we started to sell our software around the world, we would also need a great deal of infrastructure and staff development. We had to think several steps ahead as to what we would need to support this growth. And what was going on in the market? IT had been booming for years, but the marketplace was changing. There were signs of decline. The best time to think about selling your business is when things are going well, not when you have to jump ship. After all, you want to get the highest valuation for your business as possible. Now was the time to start looking based on what we had and where we were headed.

—————◆—————

Getting what you want requires you to think ahead and anticipate your needs as well as the needs of those around you, whether it is family, your team, or your customers. Empire Research, a third-party research company, reported that ninety percent of executives say they continue to miss out on major opportunities to boost profits. The reason cited? The ability to anticipate these opportunities in time to act on them.

> *Anticipate opportunities in time to act on them.*

Although seventy-nine percent of top executives say responding quickly to change is the only way to survive our current economic challenges, only one in three is even able to identify threats before they occur, much less proactively position their businesses for growth.

Proactivity means being prepared, anticipating outcomes and challenges, having a Plan B, and staying one step ahead of the curve by keeping an eye on the big picture. It's what keeps you in charge and working ON the business, not stuck IN the business. Proactivity can also help you find balance between your personal and professional life.

By thinking ahead, Wal-Mart's founder, Sam Walton, proactively saved his heirs millions, if not billions, of dollars in taxes by his charitable and estate planning. That only happens when you are proactively looking at the future and planning accordingly now.

Let's use your company as an example. Consider what kind of business you have: Is it something you have built with the intention of selling? Is this a lifestyle business that you want to run until retirement and then pass on to a protégé? Are you in the business of buying other businesses or merging? It is a common issue with the entrepreneurs with whom I've worked to have them balk at the idea of considering their company's list price. Let's say you have a lifestyle company. You don't plan to sell so you don't think about selling. But the truth is, if your company is successful, at some point someone will come to you with an offer. When you aren't prepared for that conversation, you might make a mistake that results in you missing out on a huge opportunity for merger/expansion/or sale. On the flip side, maybe that offer comes when you are experiencing cash flow problems, and due to a lack of preparedness, you undersell yourself and lose your company for much less than it was worth. This is really an issue of doing your due diligence, because you can be sure that your competitors are. Always have your books done professionally, and know what your assets are worth. Similarly, as you go into partnerships, mergers, and other collaborations, require this of the other party!

Proactivity is made up of three core elements: **Preparation, Anticipation,** and **Leverage**. These are what will pull all of your other training, resources, and efforts together into a long-lasting solution for your business.

PREPARATION

Proactivity is where planning meets preparation. Preparation is the art of taking the big picture and identifying the ways to get there and evaluating the best path.

Think about it. Our lives are filled with preparatory measures: fire alarms, practice drills, insurance, medical check-ups, and flu shots. A shocking number of business owners, however, don't take the same measures with their companies!

➢ *Taking risks is essential in our lives and businesses.*

People wouldn't innovate and create new products if they did not take business risks. But part of risk-taking is managing it. Manage your risk by considering the consequences if things don't go as planned.

Have you ever gone on a mountaineering tour? Preparation and risk management are not optional. They're critical. Before you pack your gear, you spend a lot of time researching;

anticipating the terrain and weather conditions you'll be facing. Then you gather the necessary equipment and come prepared for any obstacles that might arise. Has your research revealed that you might encounter fog, rain, or ice? Which paths would be best for the expected conditions? If you're unprepared when you go on a mountain climb it may be the last thing you ever do!

———◆———

A lack of preparation might not lead to your demise in business, but preparation is the determining factor of your sustainable success. You might get lucky once in a while, but that won't work consistently. That's why proactivity is one of the championship standards you need to employ to ensure the highest level of success consistently.

For athletes, preparation is not just doing the necessary weight training to improve speed and endurance, it's also eating the right foods to provide the level of energy needed to train and then to perform. In business, it's about your customer and your staff. With your staff, preparation means creating and fostering the right culture. Make sure you have measures in place to hire for culture, anticipating challenges before they occur so they can be corrected quickly or avoided altogether. In sales, advanced preparation means learning about your audience before the presentation or understanding your customer's needs and personality profile ahead of a sales call.

———◆———

ANTICIPATION

You have to stay on the pulse of what is happening with your target market, your competition, technology, economics, and even within your team dynamic. Staying current enables you to be more flexible in seeing what is (and isn't) working now or in the near future. Many companies lose touch with their clients. They think they know their needs because the company continues to deliver the same solution they have always delivered. Requirements and needs change, so you have to check in with your customers and ensure that you know what they really require.

Ask Your Clients What They Need

When knowledge management was the big buzz word in the '90s, my company wanted to be considered an authority to attract large companies with big initiatives in knowledge management. We decided to conduct a survey with the top companies in the Zurich area. This survey was a strategy to gain positioning in this market place and better understand what their needs were. We partnered with a major Swiss Telecom and Hewlett Packard to provide some great incentives and exposure for everyone. The results: two major consulting clients hired us to do workshops, later resulting in ongoing consulting contracts.

Become business partners with your clients and prospects to understand their challenges so you can find solutions.

Ask yourself some questions about staying current:

- When is the last time you asked your clients about their needs?
- Is your staff up to the job for today's requirements?
- What strategies are no longer working?

- Where are you obsolete or irrelevant?
- What would rekindle the growth of your business now?
- Who are your best customers today?

LEVERAGE

If you had a crystal ball, wouldn't you ask it what was the smartest way to grow your business or get what you want? The most effective way is to determine where your leverage is.

The definition of leverage is: The ability to influence something or someone in a way that multiplies the outcome of your efforts without an increase in resources.

Essentially, leverage allows you to work smarter not harder. Many people have an old belief system that when you work hard you will succeed. Working hard is often about doing things right, but we want to focus on doing the right things. Finding the things that create leverage is where you identify the right things to do.

Let's look at a business example to illuminate one under-utilized leverage point. Most people start a company believing that strategy is the most important element of their business, more important than culture. Is your business strategy your leverage? While planning is important, most companies biggest leverage point is their culture. We know there is power in numbers, that two heads are better than one, we know the sum of the team is greater than the individual. So why in company cultures is communication eroding, investment in training declining, and engagement at its all-time low?

"People don't follow strategy, they follow leaders."
                                        - Steven M. R. Covey

Leadership drives culture. At the foundation of a healthy culture is trust. It's the most fundamental and unfortunately the most often overlooked aspect. Steven M. R. Covey said it best in his groundbreaking book *SPEED OF TRUST*, nothing affects cost and productivity more than trust. When collaboration goes up, costs go down and productivity goes up. Conversely, the opposite is true. Trust is the basis of effective and efficient collaboration.

Companies with high trust outperform companies with low trust—by nearly three hundred percent. (Watson Wyatt study).

You can proactively influence your team's belief in each other through the following practices, many of which you may have already learned throughout this book:

1. Collaborative Environment. I said it before, and I will say it again: People support what they help create. Use workshops to involve staff as much as possible. As with any planning and preparation, it takes more time up front to put things in place. But the benefits in speed of implementation will be worth all the time and energy invested.

Even in the most challenging of groups and oppositions, up-front collaboration helps to get even the most unwilling players get on board. I learned this first-hand when I wanted to bring in a new technology into the market research company for which I had started to work. The company had to have a working solution in less than a year to revamp the reporting systems in order to keep the division from losing our biggest clients to our competitors. The pressure was on; if we didn't secure the new contract renewals, the division would go bankrupt. The IT department was not accepting of any new technology that wasn't Microsoft based. They made themselves clear and they were prepared to do battle. We researched this new technology and

Microsoft server architecture was years from being able to deliver a stable solution in this area. We needed the best way to get everyone on board, and quickly. We conducted a workshop where we defined the criteria we would use to review the infrastructure we needed. We all agreed to the evaluation criteria. Then we had the vendors come out from each institution and present to us. Together as a team we rated each of the vendors using the criteria on which we had agreed. Regardless of the fact that the IT people weren't happy that Microsoft was not part of the solution, they were part of the selection process, and the results clearly reflected that value of the other system. Full speed ahead, everyone was on board.

2. **Foster ownership.** People will take responsibility when they care. So find out what matters to them, and give them something to care about. Let them feel a part of the mission, vision, and purpose. Zappos has a great practice to foster ownership that begins right from the first day of the job. They offer to pay new hires five thousand dollars immediately after their orientation period ends to leave the company. Think about that. They actually pay an exit bonus in the beginning to sort out who is just in it for the money and who wants to make a real commitment to stay and be part of the team. Those who remain are more likely to take ownership because the experience makes them understand and embrace why they want to stay. Their first major decision with the company encouraged them to make a conscious choice to stay. That's powerful!

3. **Reward and recognize.** I recommend you revisit the chapter on progress and recognition. Reinforce and reward productive behavior and your people will continue to provide added value. We all want to feel appreciated. It's that simple. When you create a culture of genuine gratitude it builds trust.

4. Invest in training and development. Companies that invest in their employees outperform those that don't. A dollar spent today on training and improving your team will yield more profit in the future. You want to invest in keeping your best team members, and most likely they are your best because growth and development is something they value.

5. Live your values. Create and communicate ways to demonstrate how you live your corporate values. Review projects after the fact and ensure that you're applying what you've learned to the organization. All too often, companies say one thing in their values, but then have no mechanisms in place to demonstrate if they're being lived within the organization.

6. Hire for culture. We all know energy vampires—negative and difficult people who make the office culture more challenging. It is best to block them at the door. Create a hiring process that screens for cultural fit. Be prepared to turn away a few "A-players" because, while they might create a spike in your sales, they may also eat away at your culture and long-term success.

Remember, trust starts with you; and you won't receive trust unless you give it. Go back to the Championship Psychology chapters and ensure your level of trust in yourself is strong. Then start focusing on your role in building even better cultures around yourself, in your family, your business, and your community.

———◆———

TAKE AWAYS:

1. Anticipation is the best preparation.

2. Preparation is the key to sustainable success.

3. Create leverage for a competitive advantage.

4. Fostering a productive culture creates leverage for your company.

CHAPTER 15: SO WHAT NOW?

"Sometimes opportunity
does knock twice"

**"Progress is impossible without change, and those who
cannot change their minds cannot change anything."**
- George Bernard Shaw

TAKE A MINUTE TO CONGRATULATE yourself on your
commitment to learning the 10 Core Drivers of
productivity. Reflect on your "aha moments." How will you put
these to the best use and application? Create your action plan
now.

Now that you have the basis, be clear how you will implement these principles into your life! To help you, I created an online assessment to assist in visually graphing which of the 10 Core Driver you need to focus on most in order to see dynamic results. I recommend that you take the assessment now, if you haven't already done so, at http://www.p10app.com.

There are also other resources available on this site to bring you to the next level of mastery in these areas. Maximize your investment by digging deeper into these drivers and concepts. Allow this program to turn your productivity into profits. It's one thing to know what the 10 Core Drivers are, and another thing entirely to see how you are performing in those arenas and to take action steps to progress in each area. I look forward to supporting you further in the program and in Q&A sessions with me!

What Have We Learned?

Getting, and staying, in the Productivity Zone is about living by the 7 Principles of a Championship Psychology and using the 10 Core Drivers: Purpose, Language, Focus, Physiology, Planning, Process, Priority, Progress, Measurement and Proactivity. To best understand the required sequence of using these 10 Core Drivers they are grouped into three sections. Championship Psychology, Winning Strategies and Sustainable Results.

CHAMPIONSHIP PSYCHOLOGY

Championship Psychology is comprised of four Core Drivers: Purpose, Language, Physiology, and Focus. Improvements in these areas affect not just those four elements, but every aspect of your time and energy management! This is the foundation on which everything you do is built. In short, if your psychology isn't in order, then nothing else will be. Why do you suppose that Napoleon Hill named his legendary best seller *THINK AND GROW RICH?* He wanted us to know that the key to wealth is in our THOUGHTS. So simple, it's right under your nose...or between your ears!

WINNING STRATEGIES

The elements of Planning, Process, and Priority offer opportunities for productivity improvement by working smarter to achieve your goals. After all, why should you work harder when you can work smarter and achieve more? New and more effective systems and behaviors will allow you and your company to improve at all levels. These changes are the result of better strategies, not tactics. Are you a planner? Do you know what you will do tomorrow, or the next day, or next quarter, or next year? Start with the end in mind and you won't be caught off guard. The art of strategic planning is being clear on what is most important, and finding the balance between sticking to the plan and allowing for flexibility when the unexpected comes calling.

SUSTAINABLE RESULTS

Progress, Measurement, and Proactivity offer you direct productivity improvements through reflection, analysis, and action! When you have implemented Winning Strategies you can establish consistent, ongoing behaviors that support taking action to ensure you are maximizing your energy and achievements My favorite hockey player, Wayne Gretsky explained his remarkable success with this statement. "I don't skate to where the puck is, but rather to where the puck is going to be." Now THAT is PROACTIVITY! He understands that the best defense is to *predict* and *prepare.*

With this framework, you remain flexible and can approach your productivity with a new perspective, new tools, and new vigor. All of this gives you greater flexibility and as Darwin once said " It is the most adaptable that survive."

If you haven't already done so go to www.p10app.com to take your free assessment. When you are ready to hold yourself accountable, sign up for the accountability program with the assessment that will record your action plan and provide a resource to keep you on track and build on your momentum.

> ➤ *You deserve all the success you are capable of!*

ACKNOWLEDGMENTS

I THANK ALL OF THE people who have inspired and supported me over the years. There are too many to list, so in order to avoid leaving someone out, or making a list longer than the book itself, I thank you all and appreciate your contribution to my growth and development and the birth of my first book.

I do need to call out two people. Megan Myers has been instrumental in getting the concepts clearly in a form that is understandable and entertaining. I appreciate the many revisions we went through and even though we thought we were done several times, she didn't squirm (too much) when I insisted on another round. I also want to thank my brother, Gary, for his patience. He spent many hours challenging me to get these 10 Core Drivers from my head and into the structure that exists today. Not only is he my brother and my dear friend, but also a brilliant business mind and marketer. I am blessed to have such great support in my life.

I would like to thank my interior design editor Ellie Searl and my consulting editors, Alan Sharavsky and Sarah Coolidge for the various edits to finalize the book.

I also want to acknowledge you for deciding that you want more for your life and taking the actions necessary to learn and grow both personally and professionally. It is because of you that I wrote this book and why I am continually inspired to do more.

Recently someone asked how I would judge the level of success of this book. I answered that it is not the number of books I sell but the number of letters I receive in feedback about the difference it has made in people's lives.

I look forward to hearing from you!

ABOUT THE AUTHOR:
COACH PENNY ZENKER

PENNY ZENKER IS A PRODUCTIVITY expert, strategic business coach, international speaker and trainer, radio personality, and author. She is creator of the "P10: Productivity Accelerator Program," a time and energy management system that teaches people about the 10 Core Drivers of productivity and the essential roles they play in success and fulfillment.

Entrepreneurs and executives seek Penny Zenker's coaching to take their business and personal lives to new heights of achievement.

Penny is one of the very few business and entrepreneurial coaches who merges her own high-level success with extraordinary coaching skills to offer highly motivated individuals an exceptional resource. She is able to challenge you because she has been there and done it . . . over and over again.

After living in Switzerland for sixteen years, Penny currently resides in Philadelphia, PA, with her two children. She has experience with several diverse organizational cultures, and focuses her work on creating cultures of success within major organizations. In her spare time, she enjoys mountain biking, hiking, camping, and skiing.

Questions or comments? Want Penny to speak at your event? Want to work with Penny? Email her at P1ozone@p1oapp.com

"Stop wondering how far you can go, and start getting there"
\- Penny Zenker

MORE FROM THIS AUTHOR

THE P10: PRODUCTIVITY ACCELERATOR ONLINE PROGRAM offers the tools and support you need to make serious gains in each and every one of the ten elements of productivity. How much is optimizing and managing your time and energy worth to you?

Here are just a few of the benefits of the On-line Program:

- **Bi-Monthly Assessment**—weighted diagnostic to support action planning and more accurate decision making.

- **Bi-Monthly Webinars**—Interactive Q&A

- **Powerful On-line Training Videos and exercises**— more than fifty short powerful videos designed to further engage participants and condition new habits.

- **On-line Support Community**—Group of peers to provide support, accountability and new insights. Earn points, badges and other rewards.

- **Other Valuable Business Resources**—Access to Penny's coaching business templates, educational resources, interviews, book lists and more.

P10 : Productivity Accelerator Program Assessment identifies opportunities for growth. Take the action NOW that will convert your opportunities into real productivity gains. Join the many others who have decided to TAKE CHARGE today and join the P10 : Productivity Accelerator Program.

Enroll Today:

http://p10app.com/accountability

Want results even faster?

Join us for our P10: Productivity Accelerator Two-Day Bootcamp. Spaces are limited. **Enroll Now:**

http://p10app.com/productivity-accelerator-bootcamp/

Visit here for more general details:

http://www.p10app.com

One Last Thing . . .

If you believe the book is worth sharing, please take a few seconds to let your friends know about it. Together we can change the world!

All the best,

Penny Zenker
Personal Productivity Expert